THE
CHALLENGER
GUIDE

THE
CHALLENGER
GUIDE

Job-Hunting Success for
Mid-Career Professionals

James E. Challenger
PRESIDENT, CHALLENGER, GRAY & CHRISTMAS, INC.

CB
CONTEMPORARY BOOKS

Library of Congress Cataloging-in-Publication Data

Challenger, James E.
 The Challenger guide : job-hunting success for mid-career
professionals / James E. Challenger.
   p. cm.
  ISBN 0-8092-2669-3
   1. Job hunting—United States. 2. Professional
employees—United States. 3. Middle aged persons—
Employment—United States.
 I. Title.
 F5382.75.U6C48 1999
 650.14—dc21   99-12026
              CIP

Interior design by Scott Rattray
Cover photograph copyright © PhotoDisc, Inc.

Published by Contemporary Books
A division of NTC/Contemporary Publishing Group, Inc.
4255 West Touhy Avenue, Lincolnwood (Chicago), Illinois 60646-1975 U.S.A.
Copyright © 1999 by James E. Challenger
Printed in the United States of America
International Standard Book Number: 0-8092-2669-3
99 00 01 02 03 04 MV 15 14 13 12 11 10 9 8 7 6 5 4 3 2 1

Contents

Introduction

WHEN I INVENTED outplacement in the 1960s, I wanted to help experienced workers who were being let go. At the time, numerous assistance programs were available for the disadvantaged who were discharged, yet the individual who was not disadvantaged had nowhere to turn for help. I also wanted to find alternatives to the singularly unimpressive methodologies, such as mass mailings, executive search corporations, and employment agencies, then used to help dischargees find new positions. Each of these job search techniques was passive. Each depended on an external source to help the out-of-work individual seek a new job. People sat home and waited for a call. Networking of any sort was often deemed excessively aggressive and unnecessary for the "refined" or "competent" job seeker. In those days, it was assumed that anyone worthwhile would obviously be sought out and found by the marketplace.

I did not agree. This "wait until they call you" approach struck me as a foolish waste of time. I began to spend hours testing techniques for getting jobs. I interviewed for jobs I had no intention of taking in order to see what was effective and what was ineffective.

Eventually, my techniques worked so well that I got offers for about half the jobs for which I interviewed, except those that required scientific/technical expertise about which I could not converse.

My personal research helped me develop an arsenal of job-finding techniques that worked for everyone, no matter what the circumstances of their departure from a company were. Demand for these techniques grew as companies began to downsize and hundreds of thousands of experienced people lost their jobs, usually through no fault of their own. As the climate shifted, networking and self-promotion began to be expected, not just accepted.

The methods I have refined in nearly four decades of outplacement are the methods presented in this book. They have worked for thousands of Challenger, Gray & Christmas clients. If you are willing to put in the time and effort, they can work for you, too.

If you have lost a job or are unemployed, do not despair. The job market for experienced professionals is healthy. Companies want people with multiple skills who understand competitive pressures and are enthusiastic about seeing a company get ahead in the marketplace. Employers are looking for bright, capable people who can make an immediate contribution—people like you. However, they can't hire you if they don't know you are out there!

The Challenger Method of finding a job is designed to let companies know you are available. It asks you to look at yourself as a product seeking a buyer. Once you understand the benefits of the product—your accomplishments, skills, and talents—you can begin to seek out companies that want to purchase those benefits. The Challenger Method pushes you to create a demanding schedule of interviews and coaches you in how to sell yourself in an interview, so that you can "close the sale" and land an exciting opportunity.

These methods take work. Nearly 40 years in outplacement have taught me that there is no easy way to find a job. We push our clients to see two or three companies a day because getting a job is a numbers game. If you can sell one person out of two and I can sell one person out of five, I will still sell more if I make 10 calls and you only make one. Our clients get jobs faster than anyone in the country because they see more people.

Our firm has worked with people in all stations of life with all kinds of traits and characteristics, shortcomings and handicaps. Background and job level make no difference for those willing to make the effort. With our support, and using our methods, they have landed jobs. So will you, if you commit yourself to the program outlined in the following pages.

James E. Challenger
Chicago, Illinois
November 1998

THE
CHALLENGER
GUIDE

Part I

THE MARKET AND THE METHOD

EXPERIENCED WORKERS like you *are* in demand. In our consumer-driven marketplace, the demands on employers are tough. Customers want quality and they want it two days ago. Companies need experienced workers who understand not only how to use current technology, but how to use it to service the customer.

In this section, you will learn how to make the most of your expertise in your own industry or a new one, and discover the basics of the job search method that Challenger, Gray & Christmas clients use to find new jobs in just three months. If you have been or are about to be discharged, you will find out how to minimize the pain of separation and get started on the road to reemployment. Finally, you will understand how a positive attitude can help your job search and a negative or defeatist attitude can hinder it.

Chapter 1

....

You Are Very
Much Needed

As THE 20TH century melts into the 21st, the job market is changing. Workers are becoming more educated. In the last decade, the number of factory workers with some education past high school increased from 17 percent to 25 percent. Throughout the workplace, jobs that once depended upon a strong back are being replaced by those conducted from computerized workstations. It takes training and skill to program and operate high-tech tools like robots. Workers who do not acquire these skills will be squeezed out and forced to take lower paying jobs in the service sector.

Technology is opening the door to women in historically male-dominated industries such as engineering and manufacturing. As more women enter the job market, the number of men in the workforce is falling. In 1950, 86 percent of working-age men participated in the workforce, compared to 75 percent in 1995. During those same 35 years, the number of working-age women either working or looking for jobs rose from 33 percent to 60 percent.

In my opinion, the most significant shift in the job market concerns older, experienced workers. Once they were regarded as throwaways by employers who could count on a steady stream of eager

young workers. However, as the number of new applicants dimin-
ishes, employers have begun to recognize the value of highly experienced workers and are hiring them for jobs at all levels.

In the nearly four decades I have spent in job search counseling,
I have helped thousands of workers who have been laid off or discharged to find a new job. Along the way, my company has tracked
the length of a typical job search. Until recently, job seekers who
were 50 and older took longer to secure employment than their
younger counterparts. That is no longer true. In 1998, it took job
seekers over the age of 50 an average of just one more week to find
a new job compared to those under 50 (3.1 versus 3.0 months).
Hardly a significant difference! To me, that narrow gap is concrete
evidence of the strong demand for older, experienced employees. Let
us look at the factors that have created this demand.

Why Demand for Experienced Workers Is at an All-Time High

Demographics

According to the U.S. Census Bureau, the nation's 50-plus population
will jump 50 percent by 2006. The Bureau of Labor Statistics predicts
that the number of individuals aged 50 to 59 in the workforce will
reach 27,746,000 by 2005. In part, that is because more and more
people keep working after the traditional retirement age. Bureau of
Labor Statistics data show that between 1985 and 1995, the number
of individuals aged 65 and older participating in the workforce grew
by a whopping 31 percent to 3.8 million.

This healthy supply of older workers arrives just in time to offset
the shrinking number of younger workers entering the labor market.
Between now and 2005, the share of the labor market represented by
workers aged 25 to 34 will drop by 5 percent. The number of workers aged 35 to 44 will also drop. Meanwhile, the 45-to-64 segment will
grow rapidly and represent a full 40 percent of the workforce.

The good news for workers of all ages is that the Bureau of Labor Statistics projects 151 million jobs by the year 2006—but only 141 million people available to fill them. No wonder employers find it to their advantage to hire ever larger numbers of experienced workers!

Experience

The sooner an employee can contribute to a company's profitability, the better. In the race to beat the competition, it is experience that counts. The older, skilled job seeker has experience in spades.

Experience is a definite asset in many cost-conscious companies that have cut or eliminated training programs altogether. In those companies, management needs to fill positions with individuals who can use past job experience to climb the learning curve quickly and who can work efficiently with a minimum of supervision. Guess who fits the bill.

Two-for-One Skills

The manager or executive with solid experience in more than one area offers "two-for-one" or even "two-and-a-half–for–one" job skills that are very attractive to an employer. The company that hires someone who can do more than one job benefits in two ways: it saves money by getting two skills for the price of one, and it increases the potential for enhancing its profitability.

Two-for-one workers are especially important whenever companies are forced to cut back or combine positions. In this situation, the ability to successfully wear many hats is highly prized, and it is much more likely to be a lot found in the manager with years of experience in diverse environments.

Loyalty

It is a fact: two-for-one workers stay put. Younger managers change companies so often that corporations have discovered that hiring one is akin to "renting" a manager. By hiring a seasoned manager, especially one over 50, they are "buying" an employee who will probably remain with their company until retirement. The older worker offers almost three times as much loyalty. Younger workers may move on after four or five years, but experienced workers can be expected to provide 10 or more years of service. The fact that the employer can count on the experienced person to stay for an extended period of time is a definite hiring plus.

Good Value

Hiring an older individual, even someone who demands a higher salary than a younger counterpart, is frequently seen as a good investment. These workers have a keen understanding of competitive pressures. They have a strong work ethic and adopt a "clockless" attitude toward the workday. They understand how their job output contributes to the overall productivity of the company, and they display a real enthusiasm at seeing the company get ahead in the marketplace. All qualities that companies value!

Quality

Experienced workers are more likely than their younger colleagues to support and contribute to a companywide push for quality at every job level. Younger workers sometimes fail to realize the challenges posed by global competition and do not grasp why quality standards must be raised to survive. Baby boomers and their elders grew up in an era that stressed quality and pride of workmanship. They still see a direct link between the individual's stature on the job and in the community and the quality of his or her work. Even in the handful of companies that are not involved in a total quality effort, a strong work ethic and the ability to take pride in one's work are pluses.

Health and Youth

The over-50 individual is quite different than previous generations in the way he or she acts and looks. Today's older job hunters are better educated and healthier than those of any previous generation. They are more contemporary in their thinking, more active, and more youthful in appearance. Employers value workers who can fit comfortably into a workplace culture that includes a wide range of employee age groups. The generation gap is narrowing. Baby boomers are fit, energetic, and eager to work.

Sophisticated Technology Skills

Younger job hunters used to have a leg up in one important area: technology. Older job candidates felt at a disadvantage when competing against a generation that was introduced to computers in grade school. Now, thanks to widespread computer training and more user-friendly programs, many experienced job seekers are on a more equal footing with their younger counterparts in this important area.

In summary, there could not be a better time for the experienced older worker to be looking for employment than right now. Companies are crying out for job candidates who have the skills and work history that many older job hunters bring to the table. In many cases, employers desperately need vast and diverse experience and do not mind paying for it.

Who Needs You?

Sometimes experienced workers think the job market has left them behind. They fear their high salaries make them dinosaurs in an era when companies are replacing expensive workers with cheaper, younger workers. Or they think their job record is inadequate. "I spent too many years with one company," one thinks. "I spent too many years hopping around," says another.

Nonsense. Fears like this exist only in the mind. The truth is that today's market is bursting with companies in desperate need of mature, experienced talent.

Smaller, Growing Companies

Smaller, growing companies need you because your experience and knowledge can offer the most help in the quickest way. You bring a wealth and breadth of work experience that is invaluable to someone just starting a business.

The expanding organization can ill afford to make costly mistakes. Hiring only young, inexperienced individuals may be a less costly route, but it is a much riskier one. The entrepreneur needs to secure a high rate of success any way possible or the business will fail. One way to improve his or her chances is to bring someone like you on board so you can impart years of general business wisdom to the start-up experience.

The entrepreneur will no doubt learn from your specific industry knowledge, but it is your "corporate memory"—your business successes and failures; how you solved problems, generated new business, set up organizations and systems—that will be most valuable in making the company a success. As the seasoned veteran, you also may become a mentor to the entrepreneur, as well as to less experienced staff members. Your ideas and problem-solving skills can only help to bring a sense of security and certainty to an environment that is prone to guesswork and apprehension.

Companies in Crisis

Many companies have already experienced massive downsizing and are rebuilding their workforces. They're looking to replace their talent pool. They need you to build it up again.

Companies That Are "Decombining"

In order to reduce bureaucracy and foster a more entrepreneurial environment, many companies are reorganizing themselves into smaller divisions or spinning off smaller subsidiaries. Experienced workers like you are needed to organize the new independent companies and ensure their success.

These three categories include thousands and thousands of companies that are searching for experienced workers. By pursuing an organized and effective job search, experienced workers like you can find their way onto the payroll of such companies.

The Picture Is Rosy—but Stumbling Blocks Do Exist

Success in the job market is never a foregone conclusion. A job search is always a marketing campaign. No matter how old you are or how long your resume is, you need to convince a potential employer that you are the right person for the job. That can be tricky for the experienced worker, because even though views of older workers have been changing since the first of the baby boomers turned 50 in 1996, not every stereotype has vanished. Some companies maintain that older workers are less productive, have more workplace injuries, or cost employers more in health care and other benefits—despite evidence to the contrary. Studies show that experienced workers are just as productive as when they were younger, can contribute as much as their younger counterparts, are more dependable, and have better problem-solving abilities than younger workers.

But some employers still hang on to antiquated notions. Some older workers *do* have a difficult time getting a job. Some are turned down for jobs not because of age but because their skills are not what the company is looking for. Others are passed over because they display negative attitudes or inadvertently inspire negative reactions by saying the wrong thing in an interview. And it is possible to derail an interview. I have seen plenty of qualified people blow it by telling the interviewer how to run his or her company, or by going on and on about the Vietnam War to someone who is under 30. Fortunately, I have also known hundreds of people who used the interview to convince an employer that they were exactly the person the company needed.

The ability to package one's experience and competently handle interviews is what spells the difference between those who find jobs and those who do not. This book addresses the specific needs of the experienced worker. It explains how to find companies that are looking for people like you. It tells how to make the most of your extensive network of contacts to find a new position, and how to interview with authority. It tells how to portray yourself as a vessel of knowledge, a storehouse of information, and a terrific resource for the right company.

What you will read in these pages is exactly what I tell my clients, all of whom are experienced workers. Challenger, Gray & Christmas assists people of all ages and at all income levels—even hard-to-place, high-level executives like CEOs—in finding new jobs. When we take on a client, our counselors develop a comprehensive job search program guaranteed to result in employment. With our assistance, these experienced workers go into interviews assured, vibrant, and capable—and they come out with jobs.

I believe that the bottom line in finding a job is believing in yourself. There is no reason to apologize or be defensive about being an experienced or older worker. Employers want to hire people who are confident about themselves and their abilities, regardless of age. Repeat phrases like, "Nobody really wants to hire someone who is over 50," and you will never get a job because your defeatist attitude will show during the interview.

This book will help you leave behind negative attitudes and get to work finding satisfying new employment. It will show you how to make yourself more desirable to employers and how to facilitate a job offer. It will help you line up interviews and excel in them. It will help you overcome lingering stereotypes about older workers. And it will help you display a winning combination of enthusiasm, flexibility, and relevant expertise that gets you work.

Thousands of Challenger, Gray & Christmas clients have proven that anyone can find a job using my methods. If you are willing to commit to and practice the process outlined in the following chapters, you will join the growing cadre of experienced workers who will write the next chapter of our country's economic history.

Chapter 2

Traveling Your Function: The Secret to Finding New Opportunies

WHEN YOU ARE between jobs or looking for a new opportunity, it is tempting to consider a career change. Whatever you do, do not change careers! This advice is unpopular in an era that values growth and change. But again and again I have seen people throw out the baby with the bath water—reject everything about their previous work history, including their skills, experience, and industry—and then lose money and sleep trying, not always successfully, to enter an entirely new career field.

The urge is completely understandable. After years in the work-place, who doesn't long to try something completely different? It is no wonder many people, especially the recently discharged, are attracted to exotic options and prospects that seem considerably more colorful and glamorous than what they have been accustomed to doing. A 180-degree career switch and the opportunity to "do what I have always wanted" is alluring indeed.

However, jumping at jobs that are unrelated to what you have done before can be unreasonable and practically guarantees a long and disappointing employment campaign. For starters, you will find yourself competing against others who are already experienced in that area. From the employer's standpoint, there is little contest between someone with experience and someone with aspirations. Seeking a sales manager for your consumer packaged goods company, who would you rather hire—someone with 10 years' experience managing sales at various levels of increasing responsibility or someone with 10 years' experience managing manufacturing, assembly, and packaging operations? Obviously, the former candidate has a better chance. Every business tries to hire people with the right skills. That is why your only real currency in the marketplace is your own experience.

Time is another issue. Developing a second career involves a huge commitment of time. It is hard enough to groom skills and acquire new credentials while holding down a full-time job, but if you have been discharged and are facing a significant loss of income, time is what you do not have.

Money is the final issue. Change careers, and 20 percent to 50 percent of your salary will simply vanish. It may take five years or more to equal your previous salary. The higher your salary or the more years invested in your career, the longer it takes to equal your former salary in your new occupation.

From my observations, you are far better off in the long run capitalizing on your basic experience and expertise by either staying within your primary industry or transferring skills to another industry. That is why I advise job seekers *not* to start over in a new career, but to concentrate on "traveling their function" to another company in the same industry or to a new industry altogether.

Think Twice Before Changing Careers

Had a bad experience in your previous job or your former industry? Do not condemn the job or industry! Chances are, your bad experience had everything to do with a particular situation and little to do with your function or your field.

Black-and-white, all-or-nothing thinking leads to poor employment decisions. The premise "There is nothing for me here" may seem to lead to only one or two paths—to stay or to go—when other options exist. Instead of telling yourself, "I never want to do that again," take a close look at all the factors that made the experience negative. Were you unchallenged, unsuccessful, or unappreciated? Once you understand what happened, you can start looking for a position that offers a better fit without abandoning valuable skills and industry experience.

The Challenger Concept: Travel Your Function

Traveling your function means using the skills learned from your previous job as an immediate springboard to another well-paying job. Looking at your background from a functional standpoint opens a broad range of job opportunities. Virtually any functional-area skills can be transferred from industry to industry, company to company, or even from one area of your current company to another. For example, stockbrokers are essentially salespeople. They do not have to limit their job prospecting to financial services because sales skills are in demand throughout business and industry. Likewise, accountants are needed by all and sundry. People with expertise in computers can move into any business or industry that depends on computers for daily decision making and operations. The same applies to bookkeeping, data processing, manufacturing, marketing, traffic, engineering, and a number of other management skills.

Transferring skills is a much more productive solution to finding a new job than changing careers. It also is more productive than trying to stay in the same industry when prospects for finding new work are unfavorable. Staying with a sinking ship because you feel you must remain there is a self-imposed limitation that consigns you to a sometimes depleted job market. If you have spent your working life in the steel industry, for example, there is no reason to limit your job search to steel companies. By focusing on traveling your function, you can transfer your skills to other industries and areas of employment.

Employers, for their part, want people with experience. They regard the industry switcher as experienced in a specific line of work, although not in the particular industry. The industry switcher is welcomed as an expert and the only requirement is to apply that expertise to a new product line, whatever it may be. Because industry switchers bring with them a fresh perspective, they may see situations differently and be able to use their functional abilities in suggesting new solutions. Granted, some degree of adjustment and reorientation is required when one changes industries, but the problems are not insurmountable.

I have watched people travel their functions to new fields again and again, and almost always successfully. Sometimes a person with a speciality linked to a particular industry, such as a rocket propulsion engineer, may not be able to change industries successfully. I also have found that it is difficult for consumer product people to switch to industrial products and vice versa. However, in many functions even the latter observation is not an absolute.

When Challenger, Gray & Christmas works with a new client, we immediately look to see what skills the person can take to a new business or industry. By doing so, the person gets to reap the benefits of the many years invested in his or her particular function, while still gaining the opportunity of trying something new. Traveling a function lets the job seeker stay in his or her area of expertise without trying to do something completely different.

Why You Should Remain an Expert in Your Own Field

Switching industries but not job functions opens up a whole host of new possibilities. For starters, it is the closest thing you can find to a job insurance policy in a world from which job security has virtually disappeared.

Job security is a thing of the past. Today, what is needed to survive is job resiliency. The future belongs to those who self-manage their careers and are agile about traveling their functions to the positions in demand. Management will continue to use downsizing as a means of keeping return on investment high and wage inflation down. Even though many industries are experiencing spot labor shortages, no one is indispensable. Certain industries, such as travel, real estate development, landscape architecture, and high-end retailing, are dependent on a strong economy. Employees and business owners in these fields can see their livelihood disappear overnight in an economic downturn.

In this climate, knowing how to travel your function is virtually a necessity. It is essential to assess your skills today and determine how you can transfer those skills to another job function or industry. An accountant can become a math teacher and a journalist can switch to public relations because both jobs involve many of the same skills. The functions of these jobs are basically the same and it is not necessary to switch gears and completely change careers.

There also are ways to travel your function within your own company. Take on more job responsibilities that require the same skill sets. Or combine jobs within your function and do the work of two or more people. Both tactics will increase your value to your employer. Not only will you increase your chances of surviving a downsizing, you will be a prime candidate for merit pay, which is on the rise as a means of rewarding highly productive employees while keeping salaries and wages fairly stagnant for the remaining workforce.

Traveling a function may also be the best way to make the transition to retirement. A huge wave of baby boomers is set to retire over the next 20 years. Many of them are not ready to leave the workplace entirely and will want part-time employment. Traveling a function is the answer for people who want to try something new that is still within their basic field.

In order to travel your function you need to identify primary skills in your current job that can be transferred quickly and easily to other work environments while allowing you to work at the middle or top of the pay scale. Traveling a function means assessing the knowledge and skills that enable you to provide a service and then expanding the outlets for that service. You can enhance your value and marketability by building upon past job experience and expertise. Chapters 5 and 7 will show you how to identify your functions and find new places to profitably apply them.

The Best Places to Look for Work Today

In the late 1990s, the economy boomed. Everybody had a job. Openings were everywhere. Unfortunately, many of them were in fast-food restaurants and warehouses—not exactly where *you* want to work. For the experienced worker, however, there are many places to look for a job, places where your maturity and experience will serve you well.

Where the Opportunities Are

- Companies in turmoil
- Smaller companies
- Companies that are "decombining"
- States suffering from labor shortages

Seek Out Corporate Turmoil

Companies that are in turmoil may be among the best places to find a new position with a better-than-expected salary. In an atmosphere of instability, the company has a more urgent need for qualified people than do many stable firms. Turmoil is easy to recognize. Among the most obvious symptoms are layoff announcements, the firing of the president, multiple senior-level job changes, closing of facilities, plunging stock prices and dividend cuts, and negative business page articles.

Do not worry over unfavorable reports about companies in a state of change. Many are experiencing major problems for the first time and have past histories of solid business achievement. When they are able to get a handle on their current problems, they will have the know-how and the resources to rebound in their markets. The operating profiles of these firms may change, but they are not going to be put out of business.

Many firms that have lost ground to competitors and have undergone downsizing have to look outside for the talent they need to turn the company around. Experienced managers who have a proven track record and a backlog of experience are desperately needed. They possess the ability to visualize new workplace structures and combinations of job responsibilities. In short, they have what the company needs to get back on the track to economic recovery.

Move into one of these troubled situations, and you may be able to write your own job description and get in on the ground floor of a new or remodeled organization. It is possible to increase your salary by 20 percent or more—*if* you can convince the employer that you fill the bill. However, if you join a company undergoing change, you must be prepared to fully support the change. Fail to align yourself with the new order, and you will be at odds with the goals of the firm. That is why an important part of convincing the employer to hire you is demonstrating how your skills will facilitate change. For example, you need to show that you have the skills to provide leadership in a competitive environment; that you can build consensus, a key element in turning a company around; that you can improve profitability using your expertise in marketing, finance, or operations; and that you can communicate effectively as new systems and procedures are implemented.

The phenomenon of corporate turmoil has been increasing as companies have experienced serious difficulties keeping up with the changes in their markets. New products and processes have become necessary and the firms that lag behind in producing or using them are subject to sweeping changes in the executive suite. Keep an eye out for these companies during your job search, and you may be rewarded with an exciting and profitable new challenge.

Investigate Smaller Companies

Smaller companies are particularly interested in multi-experienced, two-for-one workers. These organizations need people who can perform several different jobs. You are perceived as a prime candidate because your varied work background puts you in the multi-experienced category.

There are plenty of smaller companies to contact. The number of small businesses (fewer than 500 employees) in the United States has grown 57 percent since 1982, according to the most recent data from the Small Business Administration. Between 1992 and 1996, virtually all (about 12 million) of the new jobs added to the economy were generated by small businesses. Whereas small companies have proliferated, cutbacks have continued among larger firms, putting many thousands of newly unemployed people into the job market. Since 1989, in excess of four million job cuts have been announced by U.S. companies. It is likely that at least five million workers will have been affected by downsizing by the year 2000.

Even though select jobs are still available at large companies, it is still true that experienced job seekers who are not looking at smaller companies may be missing their best opportunities. The welcome mat is out at these firms for experienced workers, particularly those who have big-league corporate experience. They are viewed as being able to suggest new and improved ways of doing things because of their corporate backgrounds, and as being in a position to perform several different jobs.

Despite the fertile job opportunities in smaller firms, many workers from large companies have a natural inclination not to look in that direction. The big-company person has become conditioned to the working atmosphere of the large firm. He or she is insulated by the corporate layers of responsibility and does not want to seek another type of work environment. Both the worker and his or her family like the larger firm because they feel it provides more job security. However, smaller companies are where you are needed.

Layoffs from large firms are proving the point that the experienced worker who has been a victim of downsizing has more to gain by looking at the other end of the scale. Job security, whatever the size of the company, is not something that many employers today are in a position to guarantee.

A small company is not for everyone. If you are used to the operations and corporate culture of a large organization, you may not be able to acclimate yourself to a smaller firm. If you are accustomed to multiple layers of authority, you may be uncomfortable without them. You may prefer the decision-making process of the large firm, which is often done through committee with the final approval given by a senior officer. It may be difficult for you to function in the independent atmosphere of a small business operation, where people are expected to make their own decisions and take responsibility for them.

If you are focused on one particular area of work and do not want to do anything else, you are probably better off in a large firm where you will not have to learn other jobs. If there is one distinguishing characteristic of small business, it is the requirement that employees wear several hats. An individual has to enjoy diversity and be able to do more than one job to function well in the smaller firm.

If you are accustomed to a formal working atmosphere, you may not like the more intimate work environment of a smaller company. There is much more of a family atmosphere in the small organization, and you may not want that degree of closeness with other employees or enjoy the greater autonomy taken by the top executives.

The matter of job objectives also comes into play. Individuals who want to progress and be promoted may find fewer opportunities at a smaller firm. If you are very advancement oriented, a small company may not be the place for you. If you are not particularly interested in advancement and are willing to accept a position that represents a plateau, a small firm may be a good place to work. However, remember that pay scales are often higher in the smaller organization as it gets fewer "good" people and thus is willing to pay more for the talent.

The experienced worker who can adapt successfully to a smaller firm and work at several different jobs is in a position to help the company in other ways as well. You can be a partner at the management table in charting the future course of the business and can assist in recruiting new personnel and screening job applicants. You can help the small business operator in the vital area of workplace stability. Dissatisfaction or discontent within a workforce, however small it may be, creates instability that detracts from the company's primary mission—sales. An experienced person with a consistent work background can serve as a role model to others in maintaining stability through steady concentration on the tasks at hand.

Considering the relative opportunities available at smaller firms in comparison to those at larger companies, the evidence clearly favors "thinking small" for those who can successfully make the transition. For many, it is a chance to cap a successful business career by creatively assisting in the growth of a new enterprise.

Look for Companies That Are Decombining

Opportunities for experienced workers also are growing among companies that choose to "decombine." Although corporate mergers and acquisitions continue to be common, more and more companies are pursuing a "small is better" strategy by organizing themselves into smaller divisions or quasi-independent companies within companies. Their goal is to take advantage of the energy and creativity of the entrepreneurial environment by reducing bureaucracy and concentrating on highly focused products and markets.

Organizations that are decombining need experienced workers to help organize the new independent companies and ensure their success. Within this setting, experienced workers are valued as people who know how to get things done right with little start-up time required. Your track record is an asset for any company in the process of cloning itself into smaller units and divisions.

Relocate for Better Opportunities

Many jobs will be yours if you are willing to relocate to places like Nebraska, whose unemployment rate is among the lowest in the nation. Known for its small towns, winter storms, and subzero temperatures, Nebraska is a hard sell. Faced with a serious labor shortage and a declining population, its companies are even importing workers from China to fill jobs because many people refuse to pull up stakes and relocate.

There are many reasons for such refusals. One is that we are becoming a "nation of isolates" who are apprehensive about venturing outside of the lives in which we have become so comfortable, even after we lose a job. Many people are more willing to go without work than they are to move for a job that may be waiting for them in a new town.

The fear factor is another reason. With so much chaos created by mergers, reengineering, reorganizing, and downsizing, many people fear that a new job in a new city might not last very long. If it ends, the individual is left without a safety net, lacking family, friends, and contacts for another job. Rather than risk losing a job in a new city, more workers are limiting their job search to the same city.

Dual-income couples are another factor. Many households have significant income from both the husband and the wife. Your spouse may have a nonmovable business or job specialty that cannot be found in every market. Families who need both incomes to maintain their lifestyle may feel it is safer to stay put with one spouse working and the other looking.

This trend of dramatically declining relocation comes at a time when chronic corporate change almost necessitates that people be willing to relocate. There are job opportunities to be had if you are willing to go after them. Especially if you live in a smaller urban or rural area, your search will go faster if you are willing to relocate. Moving to a new area may be your best chance of finding a fulfilling job, a brighter future, and security for you and your family. Sometimes you have to navigate unknown waters, to push yourself into trying things you might not think you can do. When you do, however, the rewards are that much greater.

If you do relocate for work, you need to set up a work-related support system immediately. Build your support system by obtaining the names of as many people as possible in the area to which you are moving. Ask family, friends, and business associates if they know anyone in the new town. Start networking before you have even moved. Call and set dates to meet with each person. Because you are new to the area, people will want to help you acclimate yourself to your new home, even if they do not know you. They also may be helpful down the road if you have to search for a new job.

Join significant community and business groups in which managers and executives are directly involved. Attend all the meetings and events and volunteer to do work and head up committees. The more quickly you can establish yourself and show off your business skills, the deeper an impression you will make. This support system will also help you from being caught off guard if by some chance you are discharged. It will help you get another job quickly and less painfully, and let you retain control of your life and your career.

Reading Between the Lines: Using Your Newspaper to Uncover Opportunities

The best source of information about companies in turmoil, small companies, companies that are decombining, and companies willing to pay your moving costs is your local newspaper. It represents a gold mine of information about job leads. In its business section, you can find clues in announcements of:

- new plant openings or expansions
- relocations of out-of-town businesses to your area
- promotions and new appointments (newly appointed or promoted managers and executives are frequently receptive to hiring)
- consolidations or corporate mergers
- layoffs

Surprised by the last item? Remember, companies are always looking for qualified people to meet their needs. The firm that is laying off people in one area may be hiring in other areas. Also, a company experiencing layoffs is a company in crisis, a company that may desperately need your experience.

There are additional clues about jobs in the general news sections of your paper. For example, your city administration may announce the building of new facilities or the expansion of others. New municipal services may be added, creating jobs. New federal government expenditures for projects and programs may be announced. All of these developments may produce hiring opportunities. It is up to you to investigate by contacting the hiring authority where you want to work and by obtaining an interview with that individual.

The Wall Street Journal is teeming with job leads, as are specialized business publications that cover a particular industry or industries. All of these periodicals and their websites will help you tap the "hidden" job market of positions at all salary levels that have not yet—or may never be—advertised in the classified section.

By reading your newspaper's business section critically, staying open to possibilities in distant states and companies that appear (on the surface, anyway) to be in turmoil, and seeking out new ways to put your tried-and-true talents to work, you will be able to generate new job opportunities. Landing a new job is a matter of applying the Challenger Method to your job search—the subject of Chapter 3.

The Challenger Method of Finding a Job

FINDING A JOB is hard work. Losing a job can be one of the most disheartening experiences imaginable. At Challenger, Gray & Christmas, our goal is to make this trying experience as brief and tolerable as possible. For each client, we develop an individual and detailed plan for moving the person from the insecurity of unemployment to the firm ground of a new, more productive career.

The Challenger, Gray & Christmas outplacement process has three phases:

1. The client assesses his or her work history, interests, skills, and values in order to reinforce self-worth (often shaky when someone unexpectedly loses a job) and determine where he or she stands in the marketplace. This step helps the person identify and articulate specific accomplishments, relate them to an available position, and obtain an interview. It also lets the client clarify the kind of job desired, so he or she does not accept the wrong job.

2. The client works with a counselor to prepare a sales/marketing program designed to sell him or her to a prospective employer

and learn the skills and techniques necessary for a successful job campaign.

3. Counselors monitor the client's progress, critique interviews, give advice, offer encouragement and support, help with correspondence and following up leads, and evaluate employment offers until a job is secured.

When these three steps are followed, at least 90 percent of our clients attain equal or better employment in their new job after outplacement.

Applying the Challenger Method to Your Job Search

This book will help you develop your own detailed plan for securing the job you want. The plan is based on the three-step Challenger, Gray & Christmas method, which has helped thousands of people find jobs since 1965. It *does* work!

Our three-step method has two simple goals: *getting* the interview and *excelling* in the interview. Without an interview, you will not be able to meet someone who can hire you. Thus it is essential to master the techniques that help you *get* interviews. *Excelling* is important because it is up to you to prove to the interviewer that at every level—social, personal, and professional—you are distinct from other potential employees who may be equally qualified for the job. Especially if you are out of work, you need to feel confident that you and the interviewer are on an equal footing when it comes to knowing how to interview. You need to sell yourself in the best light possible without lying or misstating your attributes. And you need to know how to outflank the interviewer if he or she is inclined to see a particular feature in a negative light.

Chapters 6 through 9 focus on getting an interview. In these chapters, you will find out how to:

- conduct a thorough self-analysis
- position yourself in the marketplace
- target positions, companies, and people to contact
- create a work history that you can relate during interviews

Chapters 10 through 15 focus on excelling in the interview and landing the job you want. In these chapters, you will:

- come to understand different types of interviews and their goals
- prepare to present yourself in the best possible light
- learn how to be who the interviewer wants you to be
- master tactics that make you the interviewer's equal
- assess each interview and learn from your mistakes
- determine which job is the best fit
- negotiate the salary you want

These are the skills you need to know to secure a new job. They are virtually the same for the financial executive as they are for the punch press operator. Do not worry if you have not mastered them already. Very few individuals are interviewing experts at the beginning of their job search. With discipline and practice, these skills will become second nature.

The Challenger Method can work for you—if you follow it religiously. That can be a challenge. Left to their own devices, about half of our clients are unproductive. There is always the temptation to put aside the job search and take time off. Our counselors help clients stay focused until the job search is finished and a new job is secured. Without a counselor, you will need to develop the discipline to stick to your campaign even when you feel like going fishing. Especially if you are out of work now, you need to establish a new job search routine, one that is just as regular as a job. Otherwise, you may fall into an aimless, unanchored period of unemployment.

That is not all you will have to do on your own. At our company, a specially trained in-house staff directly calls on companies to unearth "hidden" opportunities, namely positions in Fortune 1000 companies that have not been advertised. We catalog them weekly and provide job seekers with an updated resource edge in the job search competition. Combined with outplacement training, the job availabilities service enables job seekers to generate more interviews. You do not have this list, but you can unearth the opportunities yourself. It will take work, but you can find these hidden opportunities without a professional. You also can find a job on your own. The Challenger Method of finding a job works. Follow each of its steps, and you *will* find a job.

The Challenger Method

1. Assess your work history, interests, skills, and values.

2. Identify specific accomplishments that demonstrate how you cut costs, boosted productivity, saved time, and otherwise contributed to the bottom line; also, list accomplishments that demonstrate your expertise and your ability to get along with others.

3. Find ways to translate your weaknesses into strengths.

4. Prepare a results-oriented resume.

5. Develop a list of contacts who can help you identify hiring executives with opportunities.

6. Call the people on your list, setting up appointments and interviews.

7. Try to speak to the decision maker instead of responding to ads or going through the personnel department.

8. Set up interviews. The more the better; we counsel clients to make at least 5 and up to 20 appointments a week.

9. Refine your interviewing skills so you can deftly handle all questions and continually sell your accomplishments.

10. Interview steadily and unceasingly until you receive the right offer.

Finding a Job Is Hard Work

Challenger, Gray & Christmas helps clients find new jobs in a median of about 3.2 months because we emphasize the importance of attacking the job market and generating job leads rather than waiting for a job offer that is unlikely to come. We place the utmost importance on conducting daily interviews with prospective employers. Job offers do not grow on trees. They are the result of intensive, regular interviewing and nothing else.

Job hunting is strictly a matter of numbers. The more interviews you go on, the faster you will be employed. You need to concentrate your energy on the most effective and productive channels—contacting employers and interviewing with them. Checking the newspaper for new leads, writing thank-you notes to contacts and interviewers, and other such tasks should be tackled after regular business hours.

Jobs are not just found. There is no instant "fix" that can be applied to get a new job quickly and without expending plenty of effort. It does not just happen. Finding a job takes work. It takes work to inventory your own skills and preferences. It takes work to learn how to portray those skills and preferences and your experience in a manner that convinces an employer to take you on.

In summary, it takes work to apply the Challenger Method to your job search. However, if you commit yourself to taking an active, not a passive, role in your job search and concentrate on selling yourself to the best of your ability, it can be done.

Chapter 4

If You Have Been Discharged . . . or Are About to Be

IF YOU HAVE recently been discharged or feel you may be on the verge of receiving a pink slip, you need to face down and resolve a whole range of emotions before you can handle the reality of joblessness successfully. Being discharged is tough on the ego, but there is no reason to let the experience destroy you. Working with thousands of discharged clients has taught me that people lose their jobs for many reasons. Incompetence is the *least* common cause. There is no need to feel stigmatized. In today's economy, people are laid off wholesale. (Remember, more than four million job cuts have occurred since 1989.) With frequent mergers and acquisitions, corporate spin-offs, lower profits, and hostile takeovers, people who are doing a very competent job are sometimes let go with very little notice.

Being fired triggers a cornucopia of emotions: shock, anger, sorrow, resentment, even relief if your situation was unbearable or you suspected for many months that the ax might fall. Your task, once your job is behind you, is to deal with those emotions one at a time and prepare yourself for the job search ahead.

Guidelines for a Smooth Discharge

Follow these guidelines to ease your exit, receive a better severance package, and keep your self-esteem high.

Control Your Emotions

No matter how you feel when you hear the news, you must remain calm. Do not say anything that you could later regret or could be held against you. Resist the temptation to respond with, "You can't fire me, I quit." It may feel good, but it is a big mistake. Of course your pride is hurt, but the better you control yourself, the better decisions you will make and the more quickly you can move on to look for a new job.

Do Not Get into a Prolonged Discussion

Generally, your employer will take only a short time to tell you why you are being discharged. Do not get into a long and emotional discussion about this. The decision has been made and it is better for all parties to proceed. The more you protest, the more you may hurt your reference. However, it is a good idea to clarify the severance package being offered and the timetable for termination.

Negotiate the Severance Offer

Ask for more severance pay and extended medical benefits instead of just taking the offer that is handed you. You cannot bargain forcefully because you are in a position of weakness, not strength. Companies are more generous to the person who looks sad and nicely asks for help than to the person who demands it.

Forget Litigation

Do not make idle threats to sue your employer. It will make an already painful situation even more bitter, and turn your former company into an enemy. If you decide to sue, the organization has more lawyers and more money than you do. Moreover, suing your employer is generally a lose-lose situation. Suits are difficult for the employee to win and also severely hinder chances of reemployment. Not many companies want to hire someone who has sued his or her former employer.

Before you sue, consider the consequences of your action. How do you suppose a hiring executive would react to two or three qualified candidates, one of whom turns out to have sued a former employer? Even if you are the best qualified, you are unlikely to be recommended or hired if it is known that you commenced litigation against a former employer. A personnel officer with a major corporation was placed in such a quandary when a sales and marketing manager, renowned for an innovative style that boosted sales and profits, applied for a job. The applicant was well known in his industry for his professional abilities, but a further check of his background revealed that he had sued a former employer over the loss of a job. The personnel officer reluctantly decided not to recommend the individual for employment.

In another case, a production manager who applied for a job at a manufacturing company figured that having a lawsuit against a former employer would be a drawback, and he tried to overcome it. He took the initiative himself in the employment interview to explain the circumstances surrounding his suit. He conceded that he had made a mistake and said he would not do anything of that sort again. The employer appreciated his openness and honesty but decided against hiring him, even though he had demonstrated talents and an excellent work record. The employer felt that he might sue again if something went wrong and he blamed the company.

File a suit, and you risk putting yourself in the position of becoming a "nonperson" in the job market, someone no one inside or outside your industry wants to hire. Most employers are unwilling to take a risk on someone who sues. There is simply no way the company can guarantee that you will not sue again. Other candidates will be given greater consideration because they are "safe" and do not bring negative baggage to the position.

Do Not Stay Around the Office

Once you have been given your notice, box up your belongings and leave. Sticking around and letting your associates commiserate with you may only make you feel sorry for yourself and even angrier about your situation. Worse yet, if at first you are considered a pariah, your associates may not want to commiserate with you. Out of embarrassment, they may even avoid you. One way to avoid needless embarrassment is to come in and collect your belongings after hours, provided you make arrangements with security to do so.

Do Not Accept Office Space or Administrative Help from Your Former Employer

If your employer offers, turn it down. It sounds like a compassionate offer, but it is the worst deterrent to a job search that exists. It fosters the illusion that you are still working and the hope that the company may acknowledge its "mistake" and take you back. The company is not going to take you back. If it wanted you, it would not have discharged you in the first place!

There are other reasons using a company office is problematic. First, it is comfortable—too comfortable for someone whose job is now finding a new position. It is altogether too easy to "report" to the office, visit a few colleagues, spend two or three hours writing letters and responding to want ads, and then wrap it up for the day. None of this works. The only way to get a new job is by interviewing. To become an effective job seeker, you need to get away from the office completely and spend the business hours of each day in nonstop interviewing. Trying to work from a company office will slow your search or halt it altogether. It also may lead you to misrepresent yourself as still working for the company—a definite no-no.

If you think you can "hide" your discharge by remaining in the corporate office, you are kidding yourself. All a prospective employer has to do is find a friend in your old company and call him or her. The cat will be out of the bag, and you will only look like someone who lied to the new company.

Begin Your Job Search Immediately

Your severance pay is not a vacation package. Take a few days to collect your thoughts and develop a job search plan, but do not take a vacation. Unless you have a lot of money in the bank or do not mind dipping into your savings, you want to use your time as productively and efficiently as possible. Do not give yourself time to wallow in self-pity or get depressed or distressed. The sooner you plunge into your job search, the better you will feel and the more self-confidence you will project during interviews.

Get right to work updating your resume and compiling a list of contacts to call (see Chapter 7). If you begin immediately and conduct an effective job search, you will probably find work before your severance package runs out. If you sit around for a few months, however, potential employers may wonder why no one else wanted you.

Tell Your Spouse

If you are discharged, tell your family. Do not try to hide it by creating the illusion that you are still working. Confessing your situation may be painful, but it is necessary. You need their support. You do not need the strain of pretending. You need every bit of energy to focus on the tasks ahead of you.

Failing to communicate with your family is the most damaging thing you can do in the wake of being discharged. It fosters discord and tension. It impedes the job seeker in implementing a successful search for a new job. Over the years I have seen many situations in which a person conceals the discharge from his or her family as long as possible. Such a person goes to elaborate lengths to project the illusion of working by rising, leaving the house, and coming home at the usual times. The unsuspecting spouse does not notice anything wrong because it appears the normal routine is being followed. The loss of income is not immediately apparent, because the dischargee normally has severance payments to draw upon or may cash in marketable assets or tap a personal savings account.

The illusion cannot last indefinitely, however. Eventually, the dischargee has to acknowledge the job loss to his or her spouse. Anger, shock, and a sense of betrayal may be the reactions when that person learns of the discharge. "Why didn't you tell me about this when it happened?" is a common response. Imagine your spouse's hurt at being left out of the crisis—at being shielded instead of relied on. The injury is so great that it can even destroy your marriage. That is the last thing you want to happen when you are facing unemployment.

Even when you are candid, however, your spouse may be even angrier about your discharge than you are. He or she has no control over the situation and may feel additional pressure. A nonworking spouse may feel pressured to keep the household together and meet family expenses—all threatened by the breadwinner's loss of income. Although a working spouse's income can soften the economic consequences of discharge, he or she may feel pressured by shouldering the burden of supporting the family while the primary or other wage earner looks for a job. The pressure to perform successfully on the job will also be greater, now that it is the only job in the family.

Tell Children and Friends

Some parents try to keep news of a discharge from their children. This is a bad idea. If a child learns the news from someone else, the effect can be devastating. It can destroy the child's self-confidence and make him or her an object of ridicule and scorn by classmates and others. The youngster feels betrayed and wonders why his or her parents concealed the truth. When a child's faith in his or her parents is so deeply shaken, professional counseling may be needed to remedy the psychological damage.

Out of embarrassment or fear of losing status and prestige, many people decide not to tell their friends and acquaintances. This concealment is particularly true of top executives, who (with their spouse) may feel that appearances must be kept up at all costs. What would associates say if they suddenly canceled their membership at the country club or failed to show up for the annual benefit ball? Under real or imagined pressure, they feel keeping up the pretense of having a job is preferable to confronting the unpleasant realities of the situation.

Others try to draw the drapes, cut the family off from its normal social contacts, and stay sequestered until the primary wage earner is reemployed. Of course, this hiding is an immediate giveaway. "Why isn't Fred joining us for our Saturday morning golf game? I'd better call over there and check to see if everything is alright." Everything is not alright, as quickly becomes evident.

Deep-seated, even unhealthy feelings of lost pride and status are the reason people try to hide discharges. Many of us use work to define ourselves. We let work occupy a preeminent place in the way we see ourselves and the way we believe the world sees us. We define our social rank and our importance in terms of our jobs, and so do our spouses. If we see ourselves as accountant first and parent, spouse, friend, and woodworker second, we feel great shame when we lose the title "accounting manager." We feel shame when we are fired. We think there must be something wrong with us. Or we feel ostracized—certainly by our boss, and maybe by our former coworkers.

Employers no longer think that someone who has been fired is damaged goods, unless that is the way the person behaves. If you believe you are less worthy, you will convey that belief to every interviewer you meet, and your belief will become true.

That is why telling your family and friends the truth is the first step to recovering your sense of self-worth. Telling the truth is hard but necessary. In a crisis, you need all the support you can get. If you are not honest with your spouse, children, or friends, you cannot get their support and rebuild your ego. By immediately acknowledging your discharge to everyone in your inner circle, you will immediately benefit from their support and concern. You will need both as you process your emotions and prepare to launch your job search. The job search is an experience in rejection until the very end when an offer is made and accepted. Do not shoulder additional rejection at home! You need the support and encouragement of everyone around you in order to recover a positive outlook and conduct an effective search campaign.

Do's and Don'ts for Dischargees

Do . . .

- control your emotions
- negotiate the best possible severance package
- leave the office as soon as possible
- begin your job search immediately
- tell your family and friends

Don't . . .

- get into a prolonged discussion about your discharge
- file—or threaten to file—a lawsuit
- accept office space and administrative help from your former employer

Chapter 5

Your Attitude: The Most Critical Element of the Job Search

THE SINGLE MOST important personal ingredient of a successful job search is your attitude. Careful preparation combined with a positive mental outlook always adds up to a new job. In contrast, a bad or negative attitude will sabotage your efforts and harm you at every stage of the job search. When you see yourself in a poor light, your negative attitude shows up everywhere. Your self-appraisal will be negative. Your resume will be lacking. You may be too discouraged to pick up the phone to schedule an interview, and you will surely strike interviewers as discouraged and downbeat. Few people are likely to hire you.

Employers are looking for tangible evidence of your accomplishments and the intangible element of a positive frame of mind and approach to the job interview. Supplying the intangible, positive element is a matter of rooting out negative attitudes and replacing them with confidence in your abilities and your value to an employer. When you are secure in this knowledge, your search will be shorter and its rough spots will be easier to endure.

You Are a Provider of Services

The best way to summon the confidence you need for a successful job search is to *stop* thinking of yourself as an employee and *start* thinking of yourself as a provider of services. Your expertise is a marketable commodity. You were hired by your previous employer because your particular knowledge and work experience benefited the company. You will be hired again by a company that needs your knowledge and work expertise. In short, you are a provider of services—someone who possesses particular skills that many companies need. With this mind-set, your job search is simply a matter of finding the employers who need you.

Looking at yourself as a provider of services lessens the impact of being discharged. The psychological part of a discharge is always the hardest because it breaks personal ties and leaves you doubting your self-worth. When you see yourself as a provider of services, you can stop dwelling on the loss of a job and start asking, "Which employer needs my skills and know-how?" You become someone in charge of your own destiny rather than someone who is purely defined by the workplace environment.

The most successful job seekers are those who have a positive attitude. When you know you are a valuable worker who is capable of making an effective contribution, you will find it easier to convince an employer that you are the right person for the job and should be hired over competing candidates. As you hear positive feedback from prospective employers and are invited back for second interviews or offered a job, your confidence and self-esteem will grow. Armed with this take-charge attitude, you will feel confident and prepared to seek out and land your next job.

Keep the Competition in Mind

Although you are a provider of services, you are not the only provider of services searching for a new opportunity. Confidence is important, but far too many recently discharged people fall into the trap of believing, "I am the best there is. That is good enough to find a job."

This statement is simply not true. Every candidate is competing against the best. Every company is looking for the best, and it might not be you. Do not make the mistake of underestimating your competition, especially when it comes to experienced workers. You need to design a campaign that not only makes the most of your experience, but also makes you and your experience stand out head and shoulders above the competition.

For every job there will be several equivalent candidates, or at least candidates who appear to be approximately equal in the eyes of the employer. Being "the best there is" is of no value if you cannot convince the interviewer of this fact! Employers know that only in a few cases will there be clear differences between final candidates. Whereas one prospective employee may be better in one area, a second may excel in another. Consequently, the hiring decision may rest on how well the executive likes the various candidates presented by personnel. Perhaps he or she will go with instinct; perhaps on the fewest doubts. Even if you are the best, you still need to plan a personal marketing campaign and develop an engaging style of interviewing that will convince the employer that you are the one to hire.

Watch Out for Mental Stumbling Blocks

Looking for a new job is difficult at best. Many people handicap themselves by falling victim to counterproductive behavior in the job search, either consciously or unconsciously. When these self-erected barriers get in the way, the job search is even harder.

There are three psychological barriers to beware of during your job search:

- ego
- rejection
- uncertainty

All of these blocks will crop up during one of the natural "downs" of your job search. By knowing about them in advance, you can mentally prepare yourself to avoid them or develop strategies to overcome them.

Ego

Your ego can get in your way, but you cannot afford to let it do so. Even though today's job market demands experienced older workers, the employer still holds all the cards and does so until you get an offer. This fact can be hard to accept. Especially when you are new to the search, you may think, "I know how good I am and what I can do. I know my record from previous employers and no one is going to take that away from me. Why should I take a backseat to anything or anybody?" This feeling can be especially strong when you have been discharged. Getting fired hurts. It is easy to overcompensate for that hurt by overestimating your marketability.

When you let your ego get the better of you, you risk making several disastrous mistakes. You may play "hard to get" in interviews and convey the impression that the company needs to convince you to join its workforce. Or you may indulge in excessive braggadocio in the interview, or monopolize the conversation.

It takes confidence to get a job. You need to talk up your accomplishments in an interview, as Chapters 11 and 12 will demonstrate. There is a fine line, however, between self-confidence and bombast. When your ego gets in your way, the line blurs and becomes easy to cross.

Rejection

The trail to a new job is filled with rejection. All interviews end in failure except the final one, when you are reemployed. It is important to learn not to take rejection personally. A common phrase you will hear on your job hunt is, "You just do not fit here." (Even worse is to hear nothing.) Fine. If you do not fit in the company, you would not want to work there anyway. It is easy to let repeated rejection make you feel inadequate. You feel there must be something wrong with you, or you would not be rejected so often. It isn't you! Rejection is the norm.

Feelings of inadequacy are a danger signal that requires immediate attention. If you allow those feelings to build, you will hamper the effectiveness of your job search. You need an immediate infusion of self-confidence. Keep telling yourself that you will get a new job as good or better than the one you had before because that is the way it works out. When you feel inadequate, realize where those feelings are coming from, and you will overcome them.

Also, keep in mind that a certain amount of rejection is required for success. Legendary baseball players who bat .400 strike out six times out of every ten. Salespeople who can close three sales out of ten experience rejection seven times. Before you find the job you want, you will be rejected. Just keep in mind that, although it stings, rejection takes you closer to your goal of employment.

Uncertainty

It is hard not to know when you will get a new job. Uncertainty can produce nagging feelings of insecurity and indecisiveness about how to proceed. If you allow uncertainty to take over, your progress in the job search will be frozen. You may become afraid to try alternatives because you are not sure they will work out; you may become so afraid that eventually you do nothing. Doing nothing is dangerous! You need to keep moving on your job search. Lose momentum, and you impede your chances of finding a new job because it is even more difficult to start up again after stopping.

Overcoming Stumbling Blocks

All three of these blocks can be alleviated by talking with a trusted friend or confidante. Find someone outside your family circle with whom you can communicate easily. Ask if you may use him or her as your outlet for anger and frustration.

Friends can provide needed emotional support, but keep their advice in perspective. Everybody has an opinion on how to write a resume or conduct an interview. Rely on your friends for support, but rely on yourself when it comes to preparing for your job search. The best strategies are the result of trial and error. As you schedule and go on interviews with prospective employers, you learn what works and what does not. Adjust your job strategies accordingly.

The Worst Obstacle: A Defeatist Attitude

When you are hunting for a new job, you need to put your best foot forward and do all you can to make a good impression on a prospective employer. When you are suffering from a negative or defeatist attitude, however, the opposite is likely to occur.

The normal job seeker tries to do and say the things that will win the job; the person laboring under a defeatist attitude will project a negative image to the prospective employer. A typical reaction is, "I doubt if I would succeed in that position. It sounds too stressful. They really do not want to hire a person like me." By retreating within and refusing to acknowledge the opportunity that may be there, the defeatist loses the war before the battle has even begun. Prospective employers do not waste time on people who exhibit this behavior. The result is that the interview is concluded quickly, and attention shifts to the next candidate.

There are several reasons behind negative attitudes:

• People are frequently apprehensive about being thrust into new situations and surroundings where the emphasis is on their ability to perform. As a result, they may adopt a defeatist attitude to avoid perceived risks.

• The idea of having to get acquainted with and adjusted to a whole new group of work associates also can be overwhelming, causing some job seekers to refuse to look for work more than a few miles from their homes or in an unfamiliar environment.

• Negative experiences on previous jobs can cause defeatist attitudes. The job seeker who has had difficulties or clashes with previous employers may feel that he or she cannot cope with another unpleasant situation. At the slightest hint that pressure may lead to conflict on the new job, the individual backs off and in effect disqualifies himself or herself.

In all these situations, the job seeker concentrates on the potential downside instead of exploring the positive sides of the job. When you allow a negative attitude to surface in an interview, it is impossible to recover. You can write off your chances of getting that job. Employers want upbeat, positive people who demonstrate confidence in their abilities. With increased competition among qualified people at all levels, there is just no room for the negative or argumentative individual.

How to Turn a Defeatist Attitude Around

You can turn a defeatist attitude around if you recognize it for what it is and understand the reasons behind it. Look back at your personal experiences and think about how they have influenced the way you regard a job today. When you know the causes of unproductive behavior, you have started on the road to positive change.

Consider your strengths and accomplishments. Highlight, first to yourself and then to prospective employers, what you have done for previous employers to improve their profitability, operations, sales, visibility, or recognition in the marketplace.

It is common to feel apprehensive about your future after you have been separated from or have experienced difficulty with your job, but do not exaggerate your apprehension. You may ask yourself, "Will I be able to find another job?" If you left your job voluntarily, you may ask, "Should I have taken the risk?" These concerns are understandable, but if you do not resolve them prior to your job search, you will limit your success.

If you feel down and uncertain about yourself and negative about your prospects of finding another job, you will probably project that attitude. If you carry that negativity with you into an interview, you will turn the interviewer off. A job seeker who appears to be capable and confident about his or her abilities in an interview is perceived to be competent by the prospective employer.

A positive attitude is important at every stage of the job search, but never more so than during the interview. The interview is the make-or-break point for any job seeker. You want to come across in the most favorable light and not do anything that can take you out of contention for the job. A confident attitude is a must if you are to convince an employer that you are the best choice for the job. Confidence continues to be important once you are hired, for it is also important to continuously sell your accomplishments.

Part II

GETTING THE
INTERVIEW

THE MORE THOROUGHLY you prepare for your job
search, the more effective it will be. At its core, a
job search is a marketing campaign. In order to
market yourself successfully to the buyer, you need
to plan a campaign that presents you as a desirable
product that answers the needs of prospective
employers. In this section, you will master the first
steps of your job marketing campaign:

- assessing your skills, interests, and values
  to discover your most important
  accomplishments and position yourself in
  the marketplace
- mastering the secrets of using contacts to
  schedule interviews with hiring managers
- turning your weaknesses into strengths
- developing results-minded resumes that
  open doors

Chapter 6

Who Do You Think You Are?

To GET WHERE you want to go, you need to know where you are going. While this old adage rings true in many areas of life, it is particularly applicable to the job hunt. When you are 20, you do not really need a direction; at that age, any job will do, because there is plenty of time for course corrections later. Twenty or 30 years later, however, you cannot afford to drift. Gaining ground in midlife requires a strong sense of where you are going and who you are.

Self-knowledge is the starting point of the Challenger Method. With an accurate sense of yourself, your interests, and your capabilities, you can find a suitable job, no matter who you are or where you have been. When you know yourself thoroughly, you can easily identify opportunities that match your own skills and interests. You also can present yourself most effectively to prospective employers.

When you are older, there is more to explain. Your life resume is longer and more complex than it was when you were fresh out of school. To steer yourself toward a rewarding position, you need a keen grasp of your strengths and weaknesses, likes and dislikes. To land the job, you need to account for every moment of your work history and be able to present your skills and accomplishments in a manner that highlights what an employer is looking for. This chapter will show you how to assess these areas accurately, so you can improve your marketability and substantially shorten the time it takes to find new employment.

Do not try to move forward in your job search without investing time in self-appraisal. Skipping this step can lead to costly mistakes. Without an accurate self-appraisal, you may let your ego get in the way of the facts. You may see yourself as you would like to be, not as you are. You may waste valuable time and energy pursuing a position you are actually not qualified for, or chronically underestimate your abilities and refuse to try for the kinds of jobs you could get if you had a realistic understanding of your talents.

Sadly, people who consistently shoot for positions that are too lofty may be too self-deluded to give up the goal. Without a realistic sense of themselves, they misinterpret rejection. Instead of accepting the fact that they are underqualified, they persist. "That one did not work out for such and such a reason, but I know that I can get that kind of job and I am going to keep on trying," they say. Their tenacity is enviable but misdirected. On the other hand, the chronically timid and fearful think, "I know I could not qualify for something like that, so there is no use even trying." As a result, they may settle for a lower level job that wastes their real talents and limits career development.

Some people shy away from self-assessment because they do not really want to know the answers. The process of getting to know oneself can be painful. No one likes the idea of confronting deficiencies, weaknesses, and shortcomings, and that is all part of the assessment process. The more important half of the process is pinpointing strengths that lead to opportunities. When you know who you are and what you want, doors will open, sometimes in unexpected places.

A final danger inherent in skipping the self-appraisal process is that you may believe you are qualified only for jobs in industries where you have experience. You may lock yourself into an industry that may be suffering, shrinking, or about to vanish altogether. Taking the time to assess yourself will remove those blinders and reveal a world full of very real opportunities.

The Five Steps of Self-Assessment

Through four decades of counseling the downsized and the discharged, I have developed a five-step method for scrutinizing yourself and answering the question, "Who am I?" These five steps ask you to assess different aspects of your life in order to help you understand yourself in the fullest possible way. It is a process akin to looking at yourself in a department store mirror, the kind that reflects back image after receding image. I have found that this kind of three-dimensional check provides the most information with the least opportunity for self-delusion. Any distorted perceptions you may have at the outset of the process will be corrected by the end.

The five steps are:

1. Compile a comprehensive work history.
2. Inventory your personal resources.
3. List your personal satisfactions.
4. Identify barriers to your success.
5. Rank the values that are important to you in order of their importance.

This process requires concentration and introspection. Give yourself plenty of time to complete each step. You cannot write too much! The longer your self-analysis, the better. Many of my clients write more than 100 pages as they probe their work lives. They are willing to devote the time to the process because they understand that, in order to position themselves in the job marketplace, they need to answer these questions thoroughly.

Taking the time to analyze your work history, skills, satisfactions, shortcomings, and values is especially important if you have been unexpectedly discharged. It is far better to work through your grief and anger on paper than in the presence of someone you approach for introductions to contacts. I always recommend that newly discharged clients spend their first 10 days or so on the self-assessment process. As they review their accomplishments, they recover their self-esteem and rebuild confidence in their own skills and abilities.

The more time you spend on self-assessment, the less time you will spend looking for a job and the better your chances of winning one will be. The clearer your sense of self, the better you will be able to provide, in interviews and on your resume, concrete examples of your ability to make an immediate contribution to a company's bottom line.

Step 1: Compile a Comprehensive Work History

Part and parcel of your self-assessment is developing a comprehensive biography of your work life. When you have many years of experience under your belt, that can be quite a job. If it is too intimidating to compile it all at once, set aside a couple of hours over several days to reflect on and write out a history of your work life, emphasizing the last 10 years. Use a legal pad so you can jot down insights or revise information as you recall more details.

Include *every* job you have ever had in *every* industry you have ever been in. As you reflect on your accomplishments, answer these questions:

- What did you do that you were proud of?
- What did former employers commend you for?
- How did you assist employers in improving their visibility in the marketplace, market share, or profitability?

List as many examples as you can for each job you have held. Look for examples that show a progression of responsibility because that shows you were well regarded by previous employers. It is especially important to include jobs you have held in different industries. The more industries the better, because this demonstrates your versatility—a prized attribute in today's flattened, team-oriented organizations.

The accomplishments you list help you draw an accurate picture of your own skills. Nothing makes you question your own skills more than being downsized or discharged. The longer you are out of the job market, the more you may doubt your gifts. Compiling a work history that focuses on accomplishments can help you banish negative attitudes and recapture your confidence. It also forms the basis of what you will eventually communicate in job interviews:

why you are a good worker, what you have done, and how your skills complement specific employer needs.

The point of this exercise is to translate mere responsibilities into results. Anybody can say, "I have been a computer programmer at three companies." You want to be able to look at your past and say, "While I was a computer programmer for the XYZ corporation, I helped design and install a $10-million information system that revolutionized the way the company tracked manufacturing and sales information, and enabled it to increase sales by 15 percent and profits by 5 percent." The first sentence explains; the second sells you and your skills.

When you complete your work history, run it by a confidante who knows your career. Ask whether he or she thinks you have accurately captured your background. Have you left out any major accomplishments? Overstated or understated your role? Use the feedback to fine-tune your history and add anything you may have overlooked.

Step 2: Inventory Your Personal Resources

When your work history is complete, turn your attention to inventorying your personal resources. Resources are your skills, abilities, talents, and personal characteristics—the tools that you, as a seller in the job market, offer to a prospective employer. Do not hesitate to include negatives. A negative trait in one position may be a positive trait in the next one. Your partiality for working independently may have rubbed your last boss the wrong way, but it may be just the quality your future employer is looking for. Besides, if you like to work independently, you do not want a new job that offers no independence.

Skills, talents, and personality characteristics you may want to include are:

- foreign languages you speak
- computer software programs and programming languages you have mastered
- technical or professional certificates you have earned

- writing and public speaking skills
- articles or books you have published and presentations you have given
- professional group leadership positions
- special events you have coordinated
- whether you are shy, outgoing, innovative, cautious, laid-back, and so on

No skill, talent, or trait is insignificant!

Step 3: List Your Personal Satisfactions

These are the achievements, persons, acquisitions, and other factors apart from employment that have given you satisfaction or a feeling of accomplishment. They may include fly-fishing, rock climbing, bread making, or another skill that you have mastered, or a hobby at which you excel. They could include your family or your spouse, the home you live in, or the car you own. All of these are significant factors in forming the composite personality that leads to employment success.

Personal satisfactions to include on your list are:

- hobbies of all sorts
- extracurricular achievements like climbing Half Dome, running a marathon, or raising $20,000 for the church building fund
- family achievements such as a 20-year marriage or raising successful children
- homes and vacation homes

Step 4: Identify Barriers to Your Success

No one can steamroll his or her way to the top. There are always potholes and barriers. Before you can play up your strengths, you need to cast a cold eye on your weaknesses.

In this section of your self-analysis, list the barriers to your success—personal, educational, or social. Perhaps you never finished your college degree. Perhaps you are on the introverted side and are more comfortable with computers than people. Maybe you are a night owl and need a job that lets you work the late shift. Include job conditions you find objectionable, personal characteristics or traits that prevent you from carrying out assigned responsibilities at your maximum potential, and characteristics of other people whom you do not like. You need to make a candid evaluation of these limiting factors so you can seek jobs in which they are not important. Just remember that you will find them more negative than most potential employers will. You will function more efficiently when they are of minimal importance rather than thorns in your side.

Barriers and limitations to consider include:

- personal barriers such as health problems or stuttering
- lack of formal education or other knowledge deficits
- social barriers such as shyness

Step 5: Rank Your Values

The final step in your self-analysis is to identify and list all the values that are important to you in order of their importance. Why? Because values are what make you tick. If you value helping others, you will perform better on a job that lets you do so. If you value money and prestige, you will want a highly visible position with plenty of opportunity for income growth. If you value independence, you will want to avoid situations that are stiflingly bureaucratic.

While skills are a major ingredient in determining your performance on a job, values can be an even more critical factor. No matter how talented and prepared you are, you will not perform well on a job you hate or one that goes against everything you stand for. The story is completely different when your job complements your values as well as your skills. In fact, if I had to choose between an overqualified person whose values clash with a position and a slightly underqualified person whose values mesh perfectly, I would take the underqualified candidate. An individual of lesser abilities may perform the job with greater success because of his or her greater interest and desire to succeed.

Values you may include and rank on your list are:

- truth, honesty, loyalty, and caring
- change or security
- independence or relationships
- affluence and material possessions
- religious and political beliefs

How to Use Your Self-Appraisal to Launch a Successful Job Search

When you complete your self-appraisal, you will have a snapshot of your gifts, talents, and accomplishments. Use your snapshot to:

- Develop a clear picture of the type of job you want (but remain as open as possible without prejudgment).
- Identify your functions so you can generate new ways to travel your function to other industries and areas.
- Write a resume that highlights your accomplishments and will serve as a guide for interviews.

This last point is the most important. Interviews may be less than 30 minutes and resumes are looked at briefly, if at all. You need to know exactly who you are and what you can do in order to persuade an employer that you are the person to hire. You only have a few minutes to make a favorable impression. When you know this information inside and out, you will be much more composed.

Your resume and interview guide should include your most important accomplishments. Do not use this list as a script, however. Although companies want to hire people with the same basic good qualities, each firm has its own agenda, problems, goals, and direction. As Part III will point out, you need to listen carefully in interviews in order to understand the specific needs of a prospective employer. You also need to have at hand some appropriate examples that match those needs. By using your self-appraisal to prepare a list of accomplishments that you commit to memory, you can more easily relate your talents to an available position and obtain an interview. During the interview, you will be able to make a favorable impression very quickly and be invited back for a second interview.

One Final Question: Where Should You Work?

Finding a suitable match between your personality and that of a company is like finding the right spouse. Personalities have to be compatible to make the relationship work. When personalities are incompatible, differences quickly arise and manifest themselves in a negative way. If they are not resolved, you may soon be on the lookout for a new job.

Although there is rarely such a thing as an ideal job, you should be able to find one that is more suited to your particular preferences and strengths. Use your answers to steps 2 and 4 of your self-assessment to pinpoint the kind of job you are looking for. Combine them to create a list of your personality traits, both positive and negative. On a separate sheet of paper, write down what you are looking for in an ideal job and what kind of company personality or corporate culture you work best in. Ask yourself questions such as:

- Do I like working alone or with others?
- Do I like working in a highly visible position or behind the scenes?
- Do I want a high-pressure, fast-paced job or a low-pressure, low-key job?
- Do I want a job that provides a good social setting?
- Do I want a job that promises the potential for quick advancement?
- Do I want a job that requires a lot of travel?
- Do I like working with men better than women, vice versa, or does it not matter?

- Do I like working in a large corporation or a smaller company atmosphere?

Do not limit yourself to these questions. Develop your own questions that include job qualities that are important to you. Be as specific as you can.

Now compare the two sheets. You should have a clear picture of the kind of company you would like to work for and the kind of atmosphere in which you thrive. Keep this picture in mind as you draw up your list of companies to target and contacts to interview. You can immediately rule out any positions that do not fit what you are looking for, and you can more carefully evaluate jobs as they are offered.

When you know where you are going, you *are* likely to get there. By investing time and care in the self-assessment process, you will increase your chances of finding a job that suits you well and lessen the risk of accepting an inappropriate job that quickly turns from dream to nightmare.

Chapter 7

....

How to Advertise Your Availability and Not Lose Friends

CONTACTS SPELL THE difference between getting a job and not getting one. Consider the case of two managers in the retail industry who were looking for new jobs. Both had virtually the same experience, background, and number of years in the business. The first manager looked through want ads and sent out a mass mailing of resumes. With that, he thought he had done his part, so he sat by the phone and waited for a prospective employer to call and ask him to come in for an interview. Weeks passed and the phone only rang once. He did not think he was doing anything wrong and assumed that no one was hiring. He grew more and more depressed because he thought the prospects for ever being reemployed were bleak. He was right about his assessment of his future. No job seeker, no matter how qualified, can expect success by sending out a mass mailing of resumes as the sole or primary way to obtain a job. It simply does not work. It stopped being a viable job search method 15 to 20 years ago! If you want to become reemployed as quickly as possible, you need to get out there and make it happen. You need to see people, interview after interview.

The second manager did just that. Before he started interviewing, he made a list of everyone he and his wife knew. It included friends, his former business associates, her present business associates, and relatives. He contacted each person and told him or her that he was making a change in his employment situation and wanted to meet with the individual. Very quickly he filled his days with meetings at which he explained what he was looking for and asked for job leads. Meetings soon led to interviews. The only time he was at home near the phone was when he was on it, making calls to arrange for more interviews or to search out new job leads. Instead of hiding out at home in the hope that someone would notice and call with a job offer, this man made himself visible to as many people as possible who would be in a position to provide a job lead. The result of his efforts was that he cut down his job search time significantly. He obtained a job offer before the other manager had interviewed five times. He owed his success to the people he saw who provided him with leads.

To succeed in your job search, you need to be like the second man and market yourself to literally everyone you know. It is difficult to do. Most people are like the first manager. Shy or afraid of rejection, they cannot bring themselves to call strangers or even friends, or they convince themselves that networking does not work. Instead of picking up the phone, they stick to safe, nonthreatening activities like writing letters and responding to ads.

Writing letters; responding to ads; sending resumes to friends; waiting for executive recruiters, companies, or contacts to call—all of these strategies waste time on a job search. Follow them, and like the first manager in our example, you will wait. And wait. And wait. Six months, nine months, a year—not the three or four months it should take to get a new job.

The heart of the Challenger Method is interviewing. If you are willing to make call after call to line up meetings with contacts and interviewers, you can find a job within months. As I have stressed previously, finding a job is a numbers game. The more people you talk to, the faster you will find a job. You need to cast your net as widely as possible to identify the two or three fish in the sea that are for you.

By working through your personal contacts, you will be able to establish interview contacts through people you know or others who may be recommended to you. It is always better to have a personal contact than to make a cold call on a company, but going in without the contact is not necessarily a barrier. In the majority of cases, job seekers counseled by my firm schedule interviews and get jobs with people they do not know. You do what needs to be done to get yourself on a payroll!

Developing an Effective Contact Strategy

An effective contact strategy takes research, initiative, and accuracy—all important ingredients of a successful job search. Research is required to assemble your contact list. Initiative is required to place calls and visit every single person on that list. Accuracy is required because you will need to confirm the spelling and pronunciation of each person's name as well as his or her title.

There are two components to an effective contact strategy: assembling your contact list, and working that list. In each call, your goal is to get the name of an "action person," someone who can see you and then offer you a job. Unless you are looking for a job in human resources, the action person usually is *not* someone in personnel.

Calling contacts for job leads and interviews makes most people quake in their boots. A "warm call" to a friend, acquaintance, or referral can terrify those who feel humiliated asking people they know for help finding work. A "cold call" to a stranger is difficult for those who would rather deal with people they know. Although these fears are normal, you need to overcome them to find a job. Unless you make calls steadily, you will never get to interview. The more potential employers you can contact, the better your chances of winning a new job. Conducted carefully, your contact strategy *will* advertise your availability without costing you friends.

How to Assemble Your List of Contacts

Almost everyone you encounter during your job hunt can be a resource for getting you the right job: family, friends, former colleagues, individuals employed in your area of interest or related areas, even human resource managers. Start assembling a list of contacts as soon as you begin your job search. Ask friends and family to give you names and phone numbers of people they know who can help you, along with suggestions on how to approach those individuals. Your goal is to find out who does the hiring in the area where you want to work and schedule interviews with those people. If you are an accountant and your brother-in-law plays golf with the vice president of finance at the Zeo Corporation, ask for an introduction. If you are a mechanical engineer, you want to uncover connections to the engineering and manufacturing firms who need you.

Do not limit your efforts to the handful of people you know best. You need to see everybody you know. Include fellow members of professional groups; old schoolmates; neighbors; and people you know from charities, church, and community groups on your list.

As you collect names, aim for the top. You should always try to see the highest ranking person you can who makes the hiring decisions for your job function. Ask for the name of the manager or executive in charge of the department where you want to work.

Be honest about your abilities. Do not attempt to create contacts for a job for which you are not qualified. If you are an accountant who aspires to be a chief financial officer but lacks the proper background, you will waste your time and your contact's and risk alienating someone who may have another real position for you. At the same time, you should take care not to underestimate your capabilities. More people sell themselves short than overestimate. Deal from your areas of strength, where you are experienced and competent. These issues should have been clarified as you completed the self-assessment process outlined in Chapter 6. Decide whom to contact based on those considerations.

By assembling your list of sources before you pick up the phone to arrange your first job interview, you will be able to cover more ground in less time, maximize the use of your job search time, and shave four to six weeks from the process. Anything that cuts down on job search time gives you an edge in today's highly competitive employment market.

Check Titles, Spelling, and Pronunciation Before You Call

As you assemble names from various sources, some may be up-to-date and some may not. Approximately 25 percent of corporate executives change titles or positions over the course of a year. If you know your source is current and a name you have is the person you should be contacting, there is no need for additional checking. However, if the source from which you obtained the name appears to be several months old, or if there is any doubt about that person being the one you should contact, call the company's switchboard first to verify. If the name you have is not the correct person, find out who is.

Spelling and pronunciation also are very important when you are dealing with contacts and prospective employers. Suppose you are told over the phone the person who hires for the area of your interest is Mr. Smith. The name sounds straightforward, but how is it spelled? It could be "Smythe," "Smyth," or "Smithe." Find out the correct spelling. You will need to know for follow-up correspondence with the individual after the meeting or interview. Never take the spelling of any name for granted.

There is hardly anything worse than mispronouncing the name of someone you are calling for a job interview. It shows you did not have enough interest in the person to find out before you called. The contact or employer is likely to conclude you do not have enough interest in the company to justify his or her time in granting you an interview. Before you call, find out whether "Smythe" is pronounced "Smith," "Smyth," or something altogether different.

More Ways to Generate Leads

- *Create your own personal job fair.* By creating a social event such as a cookout and inviting people you do not usually see and who you know hold managerial positions, you can develop leads and opportunities. You learn about jobs by talking to people. In a relaxed social atmosphere, you can meet the most important job search requirement, making yourself liked, and gain valuable rapport with prospective employers.

- *Pursue leads through your working spouse.* The benefits of a working spouse in providing job leads through professional and social contacts have been well documented. If your spouse has a job where couples are invited to social events, you should avail yourself of these opportunities. New vistas may open up as a result.

- *Accept plenty of invitations.* Go to as many weddings, dinners, and parties as you can. These get-togethers offer you a marvelous chance to set up appointments later in the week where you can really sit down and talk.

- *Look outside your field.* Call people who are in a different industry, because you never know where your next job lead or offer will come from. For example, a financial executive who worked for an accounting firm started his job search by contacting only accounting firms. After a few weeks of making little headway, he grew more and more frustrated. He decided to call on an old friend who was in the communications field to see if he could provide any job leads. It turned out that his friend's company wanted to hire a financial manager. He contacted the person in charge of hiring and arranged for an interview, which led to a second interview and a job offer.

- *Check your local chamber of commerce* for files of contacts in a wide range of industries. Industry directories and service clubs also are good sources. These will necessitate cold calls, of course.

- *Check the business section* of your newspaper for announcements of plant expansions, management changes, sales campaigns, product introductions, and other facts that can suggest where to inquire about jobs in your area of expertise. These, too, will be cold calls.

How to Work Your Contact List

Once you have a sizeable list of contacts, start placing calls. The purpose of your call is *not* to get a job. Its purpose is to advertise your availability and convince your contact to set up a meeting with someone who *can* give you a job.

Warm up by calling your closest friends first. It is a good idea to practice making your request of people with whom you feel comfortable before moving along to casual acquaintances and strangers.

Just because you have a number of contacts does not necessarily mean they will assist you in getting job interviews. Using contacts effectively is an art. You need to know how much to say, how to be assertive but not demanding, whom to call and in what order, how to persuade them to do more than they feel obligated to do, and how to remind them about your search without becoming a nuisance. Most potential contacts will cooperate with your job search, but usually not without gentle, persistent prodding. Try never to hang up the phone or conclude a face-to-face meeting without another name or names to contact. This process should be neither embarrassing for you nor irritating to the contact. Your objective should be to keep good relationships with your contacts after you return to work.

What to Say When You Call a Contact

When you call a contact, do everything in your power to arrange a meeting in person. A phone call is far less effective. When you are face to face, the individual is more compelled to do something positive, rather than put you off or ask you to send a resume.

Do not start the conversation by confessing that you are looking for a job. If you are speaking to a good friend, tell him or her you are making a change and would like to come in and talk. If you are calling someone you have not seen for a while, say that you would like to renew your acquaintance. Say as little as possible—just enough to secure a face-to-face conversation.

What to Say During Your Meeting

A visit to a contact is a sales call. Your sales objective is to:

- convince the person that you are worth recommending to others
- persuade him or her to set up a meeting with someone in his or her organization or social circle who could be your next manager

When your contact agrees to call others on your behalf or set up a meeting, you have closed your sale.

To make the sale, you need to offer reasons you are worth recommending. The accomplishments you listed in your self-assessment will be helpful here. When you present them convincingly, your contact will be pleased to introduce you to a decision maker. If you get the person excited about your talents, he or she will think you are performing a favor instead of requesting one!

Share the list of companies you have been trying to contact, but not places where you are in the running for a viable job. (You might inadvertently create competition.) Explain that you have been trying to get into those organizations. Ask if the contact knows anyone there with whom you could speak, using him or her as a reference. If the person cannot immediately think of any leads or referrals, offer to call back or make an appointment to see him or her again. You do not want to neglect any possible sources of job leads. Some people will have information of that sort at immediate recall; others must think about it for a while. Meanwhile, you should move on to other contacts, not wait for someone "to let you know." *You* call the person back. Don't wait for him or her to call you.

If you are meeting with someone you know well, ask if he or she will act as a reference during your job search. To avoid overburdening a handful of people, you need to line up 15 colleagues and friends who can serve as references. Let the person know you are assembling a long list so that he or she will receive only a few telephone calls from employers checking your references.

Under no circumstances should you go into the facts of your discharge, your relationship with former employers, or other such personal matters unless specifically asked. If you were discharged, do not tell the contact. It will make it harder for him or her to make a recommendation to someone else without passing along the news. Talking about a negative situation also may be construed as sour grapes.

There is a fine art to being assertive, but not demanding. Be direct and tell the contact what you need. You should tactfully apply enough pressure to motivate the individual to act on your behalf, but never in an offensive way that will cause a negative response. Most people want to help in a job search; they just need to be told how. If you can convey the impression that you respect them and value their opinions, they may go out of their way to provide assistance, perhaps making further contacts on their own for you.

Follow Up on Your Calls

Not everyone can be reached in a single phone call. It may take several attempts to reach some of the people on your list. Persist until you reach your contact but do not become a nuisance. There is no need to leave several messages a day or send several copies of your resume. Keep calling without leaving a message until you have reached or heard back from that person. You may find that the person never got your resume or call in the first place. Voice mail and secretaries are by no means foolproof!

Use good judgment. Although it is better to be too aggressive than too respectful or passive, you need to be careful not to turn off a potential contact by going overboard. Also, mind your manners and send a thank-you note to everyone who meets with you during a search, whether they have a job to offer or not.

Keep Working

Your list of job leads should constantly change and expand as you see people in person. As you "use up" contacts by having interviews, replace them immediately with other contacts. You do not want to be stuck with a static list of job leads, reaching the point that you wonder what to do next. A dynamic list will help you keep your momentum. If you lose momentum, it can be difficult to regain.

Plan your calls the night before. Know whom you intend to see and whom you intend to call. Each day, update your call list of people you want to phone. Save yourself time by looking up the number in the evening or contacting others for numbers that are not in the phone book.

Start calling early and scheduling meetings right away. Methodically work your way down your list. Keep calling rather than stopping to wait for one person to return a call. If you cannot arrange one appointment, try 10 others. Develop new sources for your contact list as names are crossed off. Each contact interview should eliminate one name from your list and add at least two others. My research indicates that it takes an average of four tries to reach a specific individual. That means you will have to call some people eight to nine times. Do not give up!

Every warm call you make will bring you closer to a new job. Each time you see someone you know or someone to whom you were referred, the odds of getting a new job increase. Even cold calls help, although the yield will be smaller. Think of yourself as a gold prospector. Warm calls will put more nuggets in your pan, but calling people you do not know will still uncover them!

When Contacts Lead to Interviews

By talking to everyone you know, you will eventually begin to uncover working contacts, that is, the people who are in charge of hiring for the department where you want to work. When you are just beginning to develop a contact list, it is a good idea to practice with close friends until you get the hang of asking for and securing a face-to-face meeting. Do the opposite when your contacts begin to turn into bona fide job leads. Save your best contacts until later on in the job search, after you have become accustomed to interviewing and have formulated your responses to the types of questions interviewers ask. Otherwise, you are liable to waste your best contacts. Interview first with your more marginal sources to get some practice. Work out a daily schedule of interviews and keep to it. Remember, the more people you see, the sooner you will win a new job!

Once you set up a meeting with someone you could work for, you are conducting an interview, formal or not. Do not be nonchalant about the meeting. Prepare diligently by completing your self-assessment and memorizing accomplishments to mention. If a prospective employer asks you to send a resume first, explain that you will bring it with you. Do not offer it during the interview unless it is requested. As Chapter 9 explains, resumes lose more jobs than they gain because they give the employer a chance to screen you out if the resume does not say exactly what he or she wants.

When a lead turns into a job interview, call your contact back and thank the person for referring you whether or not you actually get an offer. The fact that something happened as a result of the information the individual provided will make him or her feel good and more inclined to help you again if the occasion arises. Do not forget to ask again for more names during the callback. Of course, if the lead turns into a new job, you owe your contact a debt of gratitude, which you should express immediately and in no uncertain terms.

After you land a new job, keep visible in the marketplace through participation in professional associations, civic work, attendance at conventions, and so on. It is smart to make new contacts, as well as maintain relationships with those who have helped you previously. You can never know too many people, both in and out of your particular industry.

Following Up on Job Leads in Newspaper Articles and Classified Ads

Although your strongest job leads will be generated through your contact list, you will also uncover solid job leads in newspaper articles that announce company plans for hiring, expansion, mergers, acquisitions, or election of a new management team. Even if you do not have a contact at the company, placing a call to the person mentioned in the article can pay off. In one instance, a manager spotted the announcement of a new executive taking over the department of a company. The manager had decided previously that he would like to work for that firm. He called early the next morning, arranged for an interview, and was subsequently hired. The first thing on the new executive's mind was where he could find qualified personnel.

Although classified ads are not the focus of your job search, they can be valuable. However, when you call about a job that is advertised in a classified or a blind ad from a company you can identify, say that you are calling about a job, not responding to an ad. Doing so will take you out of the mass response group, and you can often avoid the "please send your resume" trap. You want to be remembered, not lost in pages and pages of paper. If you respond to a blind ad, enclose your resume and underline those portions of it that are specifically applicable to the position involved. In your cover letter, describe how you fit the position.

Do not respond to an ad as soon as it is published. It is better to wait until after the first day the ad appears. Most ads attract a large volume of responses and companies often do not sort out replies for at least a week after the ads start running. If you answer later, the chances are better that your response may wind up on top of the pile.

If you spot a very good ad for which you are qualified in all regards, do some extra follow-up work. Make a copy of your cover letter and send the copy to the blind reply box 10 days to two weeks after your initial letter. Include another letter stating that you are extremely well qualified and are surprised not to have heard from them yet. Enclose another underlined copy of your resume.

With the help of your network of contacts, you will be able to track down decision makers who need people like you. The next step in the job search process is to get the attention of these decision makers. Chapters 8 and 9 will help you package yourself for the interview and prepare a resume that helps sell you to prospective employers.

Chapter 8

....

Making the Most of Your Experience

To CATCH THE attention of an employer, you need to market yourself as a product—a package of skills, talents, and abilities that the employer wants to purchase. That entails incorporating your employment history, education, and personal background into a persuasive presentation that maximizes your experience, helps you stand out head and shoulders over the competition, and convinces employers that you are the one to hire.

Before you begin to prepare your presentation, put yourself in the position of the company. Why would this company buy you? The answers are in your self-assessment. Use it to pinpoint accomplishments that, when included in your resume and stated during interviews, give an employer a reason to hire you. If you do not express what you have already done, it will be difficult for anyone to visualize exactly what you have to offer.

You may feel sensitive about certain aspects of your employment record. Perhaps you believe that your education or work background is inadequate or inferior. Unfortunately, when you view your background as a problem, so will everyone else. When the job market is alerted to and disconcerted by your concern, it will become a self-fulfilling prophecy. During my four decades in outplacement, I have obviously counseled some people who find it hard to seek a job. I have seen firsthand how perceived liabilities can be dispelled or turned into assets. You can do it, too. In fact, you *must* reframe these issues to make progress in your job search.

I cannot stress too often the importance of confidence and self-assurance. Employers are looking for positive people to fill jobs and they do not look kindly on those who are negative. When you approach your job search with a negative attitude, you create obstacles for yourself. Employers will perceive that you regard yourself as inadequate and will react accordingly. Instead of sending a strong, self-assured message, you tell employers that you are tentative, insecure, and uncertain about yourself and your abilities—and that you do not really think you can handle the job for which you are interviewing. Your outstanding abilities and record of accomplishment will not be visible when you project a negative attitude about your background. The prospective employer reacts based on what he or she sees and hears. If the individual is not getting a positive message from you, there is no way you will win that job.

Fortunately, your self-analysis can help you pinpoint potentially negative issues and work to make them positive. Review your work history and look for ways to make the most of your employment record. Identify its weak links and prepare yourself to answer questions about them. Look for ways to turn liabilities into assets. The following situations offer examples of how to confidently present a potential liability as an asset for the right employer. Use them to find the strengths hidden in your work history.

How to Turn Liabilities into Assets

Sensitivity about Being Discharged

Many people who have been fired feel that a prospective employer will think they are incompetent because they were dismissed. In my experience, nothing is further from the truth. Although being fired once carried a negative connotation, most employers today recognize that the main reason people are discharged (apart from a mass downsizing) is because someone in authority no longer likes them. It rarely has anything to do with job competence. However, you should review your self-analysis in order to prepare an answer to the question, "Why did you leave your last employer?" Your answer should be brief and not reflect adversely upon you. Your answer should not include any version of the phrase, "We agreed to disagree." If the potential employer thinks you could not get along in a prior environment, he or she is going to question how you will function in a new company.

One-Company Experience

People who spend their entire career with one firm may be seen by employers as having experience that is too narrow or too limited. Most employers are seeking people who know more than one way to do a job and can make immediate contributions to the bottom line through experience gained on several jobs.

It is possible to turn one-company experience into an asset. During a career with one company, you probably had a variety of responsibilities with many different departments. Especially if you worked for a large, multinational corporation, the range and depth of your experience with that one firm may rival the experience of other job seekers who have held several jobs. By pointing out the different jobs and responsibilities you held within a company, you can show how your level of responsibility increased. Your obvious loyalty will also be an asset.

Frequent Job Changes

Accelerated by layoffs triggered by mergers and acquisitions, the number of managers and executives who have changed jobs four or more times has increased dramatically by almost two thirds, according to surveys my company conducts among individuals who go through our outplacement program. If you are in this position, you can minimize the negative aspects of frequent job changes by presenting your background in a unified framework as a progression that shows continuity and growth. Look for ways to emphasize the experience and know-how you have accumulated through your varied background.

Be sure to communicate what you accomplished at each company. Specify on your resume and in the interview the goals you met. Discuss how you helped the companies meet their objectives. To enhance your value to an employer, you want to show that your contributions at each company made a difference.

It is important that your work record show that you were employed at one company for a significant period, at least four or five years. If your job record is plagued with short tenures, consider using a functional rather than a chronological resume. Otherwise, the list of positions on your resume may reveal or imply that you have had a difficult time holding down a job or getting along with others.

One Responsibility for Many Years

Some people fear that sticking to the same responsibility for many years suggests that they were not promotable or lacked the initiative to get out and try for something better. If you enter the job market thinking, "I was in a dead-end job," you are beaten before you start.

Look on the bright side. You were obviously good at what you did or you would have been replaced long ago. If you went to another company or companies for the same job, it is evidence that someone else found you good enough to hire. You were recognized for being better at what you did than your competitors for the same position. In addition, you have accumulated in-depth experience—a valuable selling point to an employer looking for a specialist or for someone who can help train others to do this type of work.

Early Retirement

Early retirement can be a difficult stigma to overcome. Rightly or wrongly, early retirement connotes the attitude "I do not want to work hard," or "I do not need the money." Strike the word *retirement* from your vocabulary! If you accepted early retirement from your previous company and then tired of a diet of leisure activities, you will need to convince prospective employers that you are indeed looking for a full-time, permanent position and are not merely filling time until you retire again. Your resume and your interview answers need to stress your loyalty and commitment to previous companies and your willingness to commit to your next employer. Under no circumstances should you use the word *retire* or mention cottages by the lake, Florida, or other topics associated with retirement.

Women Returning to the Workforce

If you left your job to have and raise children, you may be worried about how you will reenter the workforce without starting all over again. Before you start looking for a job, complete the self-assessment process outlined in Chapter 6. Take time to reestablish your connections with friends and colleagues in the workforce. Any woman planning a sabbatical from her profession should take steps to stay in touch with friends and business associates while she is staying home and raising her child. Remaining visible is the best way to be remembered upon your return.

However, if you have not stayed in touch, late is better than never. Get on the phone and call past coworkers. Catch up on their activities and consider meeting them for lunch. Spend time re-creating your professional network so people will think of you when opportunities arise. Make sure, too, that you are up-to-date on your profession. Read business magazines and the business section of your daily newspaper to keep abreast of new trends, company restructurings, mergers, consolidations, and promotions.

Finally, list all the friends, business associates, and past coworkers in every industry who may be able to provide job leads. As you work on your self-analysis, look for ways to transfer your skills into a different industry. Do not limit yourself to opportunities that are identical to what you did before. This kind of up-front spadework will help you expand the boundaries of your future job search and increase the likelihood that you will find an ideal opportunity.

Lack of College Credentials

I have found that job seekers place greater weight on a college degree than the market ever would. A college degree is a valid, influential factor for entry-level and first-job-after-entry-level positions where academic credentials have to substitute for experience. Of course, credentials are obviously essential in technical fields such as engineering or science. However, if you are not seeking a job in a technical or academic field and you have many years of hands-on experience, there is no reason to feel inadequate. What you did educationally 20 or more years ago is not significant unless you make it significant by saying, "I never graduated from college but . . ." Write your resume and develop interview answers that sell your experience instead of your education. Experience is what employers are looking for!

Religious Restrictions

Strongly held religious beliefs can sometimes impede winning a new job. They can serve as a limiting factor or even (although it is illegal) erect a barrier that would not otherwise exist with a potential employer.

Still, everything has its positive side! One middle manager's religious beliefs would not permit him to work after sundown on Fridays. Our firm advised him to turn this apparent "handicap" to his advantage by offering to work on Sundays instead. It worked, and he was quickly employed. Two years later, he had only worked on three Sundays in all that time.

Physical Challenges

Today's job market has room for everybody, even people who are physically challenged. For example, a middle manager who had been with her previous employer for nine years had a great deal of expertise with computers. However, she was no longer able to do her work because of failing eyesight. With my firm's support and counseling, she traveled her function by starting her own business teaching computer skills to children. It offered her a way to use her skills indirectly while remaining in her field.

Another middle manager had a severe stuttering problem which was aggravated by the shock of being discharged. He could not carry on a telephone conversation and could barely speak without stuttering. However, he was an excellent tax accountant who had worked for his previous employer for many years. We counseled him to investigate the least threatening situations in his job search and to go only to people who knew him and were aware of his expertise. The strategy worked; within three months he was employed.

Many people with profound physical disabilities are employed as inside salespeople and technical and customer service specialists. Advanced computer and telecommunications equipment makes it possible for them to answer phone calls, handle correspondence, and carry out all the duties associated with the job. If you are physically challenged, play up your strengths and minimize your challenges by seeking out positions where your talents can shine.

Chief Executive Officers and Other Top Executives

To the man on the street, it would seem that all doors would open to the CEO or top executive seeking a new position. Not so. Surprisingly, these executives can have a very difficult time finding a new job. For one thing, there are fewer jobs the higher one ascends on the job pyramid. For another, the top executive's contacts tend to be other highly placed executives. It is difficult for one CEO to approach another about a job, because the employed CEO often has the position the job seeker wants. Since the incumbent CEO is not about to leave, the job-seeking CEO must either accept a lower level job or look elsewhere. The same situation holds true for vice presidents, division heads, and others at the top.

Even a lower level job can be difficult to find. The CEO may be rejected because no one wants to hire an executive who may be contemplating taking over the existing CEO's job. Also, few believe that someone who has enjoyed the power and privileges of the top job would willingly take a step or two down.

A final hurdle concerns power and control. Top executives are accustomed to running operations and making the ultimate decisions. During a job search, the hiring company is the decision maker that controls the process and has the power. This lack of power can be very uncomfortable for the former executive.

If you were previously an executive at the top of your former company, how can you turn these perceived liabilities into strengths? Like other job seekers, you need to sell your accomplishments—how you cut costs, reduced overhead, saved time, and so forth. More important, you need to stress that you are a team player. Demonstrate that you did not reign over your kingdom but actively sought out the advice and counsel of others in order to ensure that the goals of the company were achieved. Give specific examples that show how you motivated employees, and how you set the tone and led in a manner that others wanted to follow. Most important of all, you need to show how you made a positive impact on the company. With these points stressed, doors *will* open to you once again.

What Is Your Liability?

What trait holds you back? Working through your self-assessment should have alerted you to potential liabilities. Go back through what you have written and identify these areas. Follow the preceding examples and find ways to give them the best possible spin. When you have found the strength hidden in the liability, you will be ready to draft your resume and prepare your answers to interview questions. Properly presented, your career history is a testimony to the fact that you are a hard-working, self-motivated person who can make an immediate and positive impact on the company's bottom line.

Chapter 9

··

The Resume Is
Not a Brochure

A RESUME ALONE will not get you a job. It is not a brochure that can speak for you. It may not even open any doors! Most employers use resumes to *eliminate* candidates for a job. You may be eliminated from the recruitment process without ever having an interview if there is something in your resume that the employer does not like or feels is missing.

However, a well-written resume can provide enough information to interest the employer in interviewing you. While it is no substitute for an interview, your resume should be prepared in such a manner that it will stand on its own and provide enough information about you to enable an employer to make an intelligent decision. Remember, all candidates being considered look alike. Your resume needs to present your accomplishments and capabilities in a manner that makes you stand out over the competition and catches the employer's attention.

Three Kinds of Resumes

Challenger, Gray & Christmas recommends three types of resumes for its clients:

- short chronological resume
- long chronological resume
- functional resume

Each one has a different appearance and a different purpose.

Short Chronological Resume

A short chronological resume summarizes the last 10 years of your career in reverse, briefly listing your accomplishments from the most recent to the much older. Figure 9.1 shows how one sales and marketing executive summarized 22 years of experience in just two pages. (Even though the resumes shown on pages 79-84 are each spread over three pages in out text, they should fill two standard 8½ by 11″ sheets of paper). A short chronological resume summarizes the last 10 years. This type of resume should be used whenever you are forced to go through a screening process instead of going to a decision maker.

Brevity is important, because many firms still sort through resumes manually. Your short chronological resume should contain enough information to get you into the "will interview" pile, but not so much that it overwhelms the individual sifting through a high pile of resumes.

Increasing numbers of search firms, executive recruiters, and personnel managers initially use computer software to scan resumes history, education, location, and so forth. Once scanned, resumes can be sorted by these key words to produce a customized list of professionals in a certain field. By including the right key words in your short chronological resume, you can increase the chances that it will pass the screen.

As for content, while accomplishments are paramount, you should also stress responsibilities, position titles, and your education. For example, although it does not contain as much detail as a long chronological resume, the short resume in Figure 9.2 summarizes the applicant's ability to make bottom-line contributions to an employer.

Veronica Littleton
7444 Coeur d'Alene Avenue
Boise, Idaho 99222
(208) 555-7721

A Summary: I am a sales and marketing executive with a solid background in sales operations, sales administration, systems marketing, systems planning, and channel sales. My skills include: developing and implementing strategies; closing complex negotiations and sales; building strong professional partner relationships; and speaking to industry groups, press, and analysts. Achievements include:

B ■ Channel Sales: Established/maintained sales and marketing relationships with 10+ Pan-American distributors. Recruited 2,000 resellers. Delivered executive-level customer presentations. Participated in distributor and reseller training. Developed educational and government channel sales programs. Set up employee purchase programs. Liquidated remaining systems inventory. Developed programs and negotiated the liquidation of remaining systems inventory.

■ Systems Marketing: Organized focus groups and market research for the corporate systems and distribution channel. Wrote positioning statements and key sales messages. Developed reseller and field sales lead management systems. Created sales programs and sales tools for distribution channel and field sales teams. Designed CD-ROM–based reseller training tools, direct mail recruitment, and sales programs. Coordinated distributor and reseller programs and program guides.

■ Systems Planning: Created a strategy for the distribution of commercial computer systems. Developed plans for the introduction and launch of Lightman products. Planned the termination of distributor relationships and the closing of the business.

■ Sales Administration: Developed and negotiated distributor/reseller contracts. Staffed a sales and operations organization, provided career development and appraisals. Maintained departmental budgets and expense controls. Consolidated sales territories. Presented sales/operational status at monthly executive reviews. Developed and reconciled monthly sales forecasts. Developed allocation methodology for high demand products. Implemented an incentive sales plan for the channel sales team.

■ Sales Operations: Created a distributor/reseller co-op program. Established a commercial DOA policy. Instituted price protection policies

Figure 9.1   Short Chronological Resume #1

A By leading off with an extensive summary of her experience, this short chronological resume positions Ms. Littleton as a sales and marketing executive with wide experience and a solid track record.

B For each of her previous positions, Ms. Littleton provides a summary of her responsibilities and accomplishments. Phrases like "Recruited 2,000 resellers" quantify her accomplishments and their value to her former employers.

and programs. Developed a customer evaluation program. Set up a reseller demonstration program. Formulated stock rotation prices and procedures.

Education: Drake University, Des Moines, Iowa, 1990
Master of Business Administration - Marketing

Oklahoma State University, Oklahoma City, Oklahoma, 1983
Bachelor of Science - Management

Experience: **XONAX CORPORATION**   Boise, Idaho

Director, Worldwide Channel Development   **1994–1998**

Directed and planned all aspects of the development and implementation for Pan-American distribution of the computer group's Power PC products. Developed and implemented worldwide distribution strategy and programs which enabled the company to successfully launch and sell commercially branded systems through a volume-based distribution model.

Managed distribution sales activities across multiple geographic territories. Negotiated strategic distribution relationships with major U.S., Canadian, and Latin American distributors. Led a staff of senior sales managers responsible for selling and implementation of marketing plans/promotions, product transitions, and inventory management.

**COMPRO COMPUTER
CORPORATION**   San Leandro, California

**Department Manager, North American
Systems Marketing**   **1990–1994**

Directed marketing activities for the line of company servers, networking products, and management software. Developed a staff of senior marketing professionals in the operation and execution of marketing plans/promotions, product announcements, and inventory/life cycle management.

Ⓒ ────── Increased server products, a $1,000,000,000 business, by 82% in one year. Created improved distribution strategies, enabling the company to enter the direct mail and retail markets. Produced and implemented a marketing communication and advertising program which heightened company image.

Figure 9.1   Short Chronological Resume #1 continued

C   Impressive results like this 82 percent increase in sales are highlighted wherever possible.

SPHERE COMPUTER, INC.   Lexington, Massachusetts

Department Manager, Communications/Networking
Marketing   **1986–1990**

Responsible for the marketing and project management of the company's proprietary and UNIX-based communications and networking hardware and software products. Directed a staff of product managers in business and product planning for a variety of communications products and protocols.

Developed the corporate communications strategic plan. Prepared business plans including marketing strategy, product definition, product/market requirements, and competitive analysis. Negotiated strategic product relationships with IBM, AT&T, and other major distributors.

FCB FINANCIAL SYSTEMS   Boston, Massachusetts

Manager/Project Manager   **1979–1986**

Managed an advanced technology group chartered to increase productivity in credit/collections. Led a team of developers supporting large CICS applications, including a worldwide messaging system, a network billing and inventory system, and a document/office automation system.

Designed call distribution systems utilizing PBX, IBM mainframes, AT&T 3B2's (UNIX), and fault tolerant systems. Directed activities in the design and implementation of a European communications control center. Coordinated project requirements with international users, government agencies, and domestic operations.

**Additional
Experience:** *Liverpool Insurance Company*, Boston, Massachusetts. Systems Programmer/Applications Analyst, 1978–1979. Developed a prospective insurance agent system, and supported vendor-supplied communication software. *Pacific Gas & Electric Company*, Sacramento, California. Programmer, 1976–1978. Supported various applications including customer activity, property accounting, and stock ownership.

Personal: Enjoy sports such as tennis and golf; playing the violin; traveling internationally.

Figure 9.1   Short Chronological Resume #1 continued

D   Additional experience is mentioned briefly along with personal data.

Melvin R. Smith
7210 Days Creek Road
Lexington, KY 40501
(606) 555-1234

Qualifications

As a financial executive and CPA, my areas of expertise include accounting, systems implementation, finance, administration, computer integration, computer programming, network administration, real estate development, land acquisition, construction, cash management, property management, human resources, and executive functions. I saved substantial amounts of money on accounting fees. I designed and/or implemented accounting, time and billing, docketing/case management, and other systems. I refinanced a 200,000-square-foot shopping center, generating several million dollars.

I analyzed many properties for acquisition and prepared pro forma statements to obtain financing. I administered lease contracts and qualified retirement plans. I designed, installed, and administered a 50 note Novell Netware 3.11 network. I also managed major renovations, build outs, and expansions. At the personal level, I am able to sell my ideas and build consensus. I love problems and am a creative person, while also a sound decision maker. I am able to distill information for presentation to others. I am also even-tempered and tenacious.

Experience

SOUTHERN DEVELOPMENT CORPORATION   Lexington, Kentucky

CHIEF FINANCIAL OFFICER, 1997

Oversaw all financial responsibilities for a small company involved in various real estate activities, as well as over 50 related entities that were mostly individual real estate investments. The company was essentially a start-up operation relative to the real estate development side of the operation. Handled all financial aspects of the company's acquisition of land and its subsequent development for manufactured housing communities. Established policies and procedures.

Implemented a new and significantly better accounting and reporting system for the company and all related entities using Timberline Gold 4.x. Organized the historical records of the company. Further, made preparations to have the company become a manufactured household dealer; investigated the setting up of a joint venture with a bank or mortgage company to begin originating and servicing mortgages on the manufactured housing units that the company would sell. In addition, supported the pretrial settlement of a case for a company-related entity worth a potential of $15,000,000.

Figure 9.2   Short Chronological Resume #2

LOMBARD, MADISON, AND FLECK, PPLC   Lexington, Kentucky

EXECUTIVE DIRECTOR OF ADMINISTRATION, 1990–1997

Ran all of the day-to-day operations of the firm. Was responsible for all accounting and finance functions of the firm. In addition, oversaw the implementation, maintenance, and administration of the firm's computer system. Was a trustee of the firm's profit-sharing 401(k) plan. Was also chairman of the firm's executive committee, and chaired the general partnership meetings.

Personally created and installed a LAN, saving $100,000 in installation costs, and provided all necessary repairs and maintenance. Set up a computerized accounting system, a time and billing software package, and a docketing system compatible with the software. Provided secretaries with scanning technology. Took over most accounting functions from an outside CPA firm, saving $33,000 a year. Restructured the compensation formula to satisfy a maximum number of employees. Resolved merger issues, saving the firm as much as $300,000 on the purchase of a branch office. Created a 401(k) plan as well.

SAMUEL ROSCOE ASSOCIATES, INC.   Lexington, Kentucky

CHIEF FINANCIAL OFFICER, 1986–1990

Ran the day-to-day operations of the firm, handling all of the accounting, finance, and treasury functions. Also managed the operation and maintenance of the company's headquarters, which it owned. Oversaw the firm's administrative and clerical staff of ten. Was a trustee of the firm's profit-sharing plan and 401(k) plan, which I implemented.

Obtained new accounting software for general ledger, accounts payable/receivable, billing, and payroll. Installed a Novell network, and introduced WordPerfect and AutoCad. Replaced unnecessary, $100,000 full audits with a $20,000 'review.' Created and administered formal project management systems, and compiled a database of project information. During a difficult period for the firm, handled cash management, including collections and vendor relations, and never missed a payroll.

Previous Employment

Swarthmore-Miles Company, Louisville, Kentucky - Controller/Project Manager, 1982–1985. *Cavin Transfer Incorporated*, Cincinnati, Ohio - Controller, 1980–1982. *Sablan International Forwarding, Inc.*, Cincinnati, Ohio - Director and Treasurer, 1980–1982 (concurrent and related to employment with Cavin Transfer Incorporated).

Lundby, Jones & Company, P.C., Cleveland, Ohio - CPA, Senior Accountant, 1977–1980. *Brown, McPhail and Grady*, Cleveland, Ohio - In-Charge Accountant, 1976–1977. *Ernst & Young (formerly Ernst & Whinney)*, Sandusky, Ohio - In-Charge Accountant/Staff Accountant, 1974–1976.

Figure 9.2   Short Chronological Resume #2, continued

Education

Miami University of Ohio, Oxford, Ohio
M.B.A. 1974, Finance

University of Ohio, Athens, Ohio
B.S. 1972, Architecture

Personal

Certifications: Real Estate License - Kentucky, 1985; CPA - Ohio, 1977.
Memberships: American Institute of Certified Public Accountants; Kentucky Association of Certified Public Accountants; Annual Fund Chair, Miami University Class of '74.

Figure 9.2   Short Chronological Resume #2, continued

Long Chronological Resume

Use the long chronological resume when you meet with the hiring decision maker. Its goal is to distinguish you from other contenders whose backgrounds resemble yours. To do so, focus on accomplishments, not responsibilities. In Figures 9.3 and 9.4, the executives profiled in Figures 9.1 and 9.2, provide a comprehensive summary of their career accomplishments.

Your path to divisional sales manager may not be unique; chances are most divisional sales managers started out as sales representatives and put in a few years as sales managers before ascending to divisional manager. Moreover, most divisional managers will content themselves with a basic chronological resume. To set yourself apart from the competition, provide details about what you did to earn each promotion. Did you win every sales contest during your first five years in the business? Say so. Did sales in your division double under your leadership? Put it on paper. Include all your major milestones for the previous five to ten years.

Companies want to hire people who are good at what they do. You can alert them to your strengths by starting your resume with a paragraph or two that positions you in the marketplace by summarizing your experience.

Veronica Littleton
7444 Coeur d'Alene Avenue
Boise, Idaho 99222
(208) 555-7721

Summary: I am a sales and marketing executive with a solid background in sales operations, sales administration, systems marketing, systems planning, and channel sales. My skills include: developing and implementing strategies; closing complex negotiations and sales; building strong professional partner relationships; and speaking to industry groups, press, and analysts. Achievements include:

- Channel Sales: Established/maintained sales and marketing relationships with 10+ Pan-American distributors. Recruited 2,000 resellers. Delivered executive-level customer presentations. Participated in distributor and reseller training. Developed educational and government channel sales programs. Set up employee purchase programs. Liquidated remaining systems inventory. Developed programs and negotiated the liquidation of remaining systems inventory.

- Systems Marketing: Organized focus groups and market research for the corporate systems and distribution channel. Wrote positioning statements and key sales messages. Developed reseller and field sales lead management systems. Created sales programs and sales tools for distribution channel and field sales teams. Designed CD-ROM–based reseller training tools, direct mail recruitment, and sales programs. Coordinated distributor and reseller programs and program guides.

- Systems Planning: Created a strategy for the distribution of commercial computer systems. Developed plans for the introduction and launch of Lightman products. Planned the termination of distributor relationships and the closing of the business.

- Sales Administration: Developed and negotiated distributor/reseller contracts. Staffed a sales and operations organization, provided career development and appraisals. Maintained departmental budgets and expense controls. Consolidated sales territories. Presented sales/operational status at monthly executive reviews. Developed and reconciled monthly sales forecasts. Developed allocation methodology for high demand products. Implemented an incentive sales plan for the channel sales team.

- Sales Operations: Created a distributor/reseller co-op program. Established a commercial DOA policy. Instituted price protection policies and programs. Developed a customer evaluation program. Set up a reseller demonstration program. Formulated stock rotation prices and procedures.

Figure 9.3   Long Chronological Resume #1

A   For her long chronological resume, Ms. Littleton repeats the introductory summary but provides extensive detail about her responsibilities and accomplishments on each job.

Education: Drake University, Des Moines, Iowa, 1990
             Master of Business Administration - Marketing

             Oklahoma State University, Oklahoma City, Oklahoma, 1983
             Bachelor of Science - Management

B — Experience: XONAX CORPORATION   Boise, Idaho

             Director, Worldwide Channel Development   1994–1998

             Directed and planned all aspects of the development and imple-
             mentation for Pan-American distribution of the computer group's
             Power PC products. Developed and implemented worldwide dis-
             tribution strategy and programs which enabled the company to
             successfully launch and sell commercially branded systems
             through a volume-based distribution model.

             Managed distribution sales activities across multiple geographic
             territories. Negotiated strategic distribution relationships with
             major U.S., Canadian, and Latin American distributors. Led a
             staff of senior sales managers responsible for selling and imple-
             mentation of marketing plans/promotions, product transitions,
             and inventory management.

C —   • **WORLDWIDE CHANNEL PROGRAMS:** Researched and
               developed a worldwide channel strategy enabling the company
               to launch commercial Power PC products targeted at the AIX,
               NT, and MAC OS market. Developed and executed worldwide
               channel programs, both strategic and tactical, to ensure pene-
               tration of Lightman market share.

                 • Administration - Directed and managed the sales process
                   and channel sales team, including forecast, bookings,
                   billings, and revenue reporting. Established and managed
                   budgets and expenses for the department in launching a
                   North American channel sales organization and world-
                   wide channel programs.

                 • Development of External Relations - Built and solidified
                   relationships with channel partners, key consultants, ana-
                   lysts, and the press, providing effective communication of
                   strategies and key messages.

                   Maintained executive relationships with the channel part-
                   ners, advising them on strategic plans, directional

Figure 9.3   Long Chronological Resume #1 continued

B   Each position is summarized in a paragraph or two.

C   For each area of responsibility, Ms. Littleton details how she built business and increased revenues and profits.

changes, and customer relations. Enacted operational policies and procedures enabling the company and its channel partners to conduct business using a two-tiered commercial distribution model.

- Development and Implementation of Marketing Plans - Directed and managed the planning and implementation of all channel marketing programs, including strategies, budgets, personnel, and outside services, ensuring effective and timely utilization of resources.

- STRATEGIC PLANNING: Coordinated with the group general manager and executive management team on the state of the business, forecast and sales plans, marketing and pricing initiatives, and strategic partner negotiations. Established and maintained sales and territory plans for the U.S., Canada, and Latin America. Created programs for price protection, stock rotation/balancing, DOC returns, and marketing fund accruals and allocations.

- MANAGEMENT OF RESELLERS AND DISTRIBUTORS: Directed customer and reseller market research activities, including focus groups, blind customer surveys, and discussion teams. Arranged direct distributor and reseller training, including instructor lead classes, video and interactive training, and hands-on early evaluation programs.

  Developed and negotiated contracts for distribution partners and resellers. Led recruitment activities for targeted resellers based on key criteria to establish coverage, competition, and support for the emerging customer base.

- BUILDING OF PARTNER AND ACCOUNT RELATIONS: Oversaw the relationships and activities for outsourced partners for telemarketing, interactive training, lead management, and co-op reporting/processing. Built and maintained relationships with national accounts, coordinating marketing, advertising, PR, and direct sales activities.

- SUPPORT OF PRODUCT DEVELOPMENT: Interfaced with other functional divisions, such as product management, development, service, and finance, in the positioning, launching, and pricing of products in the marketplace.

- TEAM BUILDING/HUMAN RESOURCES: Directed all channel staffing and staff development activities, ensuring that a cohesive team was formulated and the staff was gaining efficiencies. Enhanced the individuals' career goals, as well.

Figure 9.3   Long Chronological Resume #1 continued

Developed channel territory and commission plans in order to motivate and compensate the business development managers.

COMPRO COMPUTER CORPORATION San Leandro, California

Department Manager, North American Systems Marketing
                                                    1990–1994

Directed marketing activities for the line of company servers, networking products, and management software. Developed a staff of senior marketing professionals in the operation and execution of marketing plans/promotions, product announcements, and inventory/life cycle management.

Increased server products, a $1,000,000,000 business, by 82% in one year. Created improved distribution strategies, enabling the company to enter the direct mail and retail markets. Produced and implemented a marketing communication and advertising program which heightened company image.

- **82% INCREASE OF SERVER BUSINESS:** Developed the marketing and distribution strategies for corporate server products within North America. This business was worth nearly $1,000,000,000. Generated an increase of 82% from the previous year.

- **EXPANSION OF DISTRIBUTION CAPABILITIES:** Implemented broad-scale distribution strategies which enhanced the company's presence as a high-end systems manufacturer. The plans launched the company's systems entrée in direct mail and retail.

- **MARKETING COMMUNICATION AND ADVERTISING:** Coordinated the development and implementation of a comprehensive marketing communication and advertising program. It enhanced the company's image as a leader in network computing.

SPHERE COMPUTER, INC.   Lexington, Massachusetts

Department Manager, Communications/Networking Marketing
                                                    1986–1990

Figure 9.3   *Long Chronological Resume #1 continued*

D Bullets highlight outstanding results such as an 82 percent increase in sales and a project that enabled the company to enter a new market.

E Jobs held more than nine years ago get a thorough but shorter description.

Responsible for the marketing and project management of the company's proprietary and UNIX-based communications and networking hardware and software products. Directed a staff of product managers in business and product planning for a variety of communications products and protocols.

Developed the corporate communications strategic plan. Prepared business plans including marketing strategy, product definition, product/market requirements, and competitive analysis. Negotiated strategic product relationships with IBM, AT&T, and other major distributors.

FCB FINANCIAL SYSTEMS   Boston, Massachusetts

Manager/Project Manager   1979–1986

Managed an advanced technology group chartered to increase productivity in credit/collections. Led a team of developers supporting large CICS applications, including a worldwide messaging system, a network billing and inventory system, and a document/office automation system.

Designed call distribution systems utilizing PBX, IBM mainframes, AT&T 3B2's (UNIX), and fault tolerant systems. Directed activities in the design and implementation of a European communications control center. Coordinated project requirements with international users, government agencies, and domestic operations.

Additional Experience: *Liverpool Insurance Company*, Boston, Massachusetts. Systems Programmer/Applications Analyst, 1978–1979. Developed a prospective insurance agent system, and supported vendor-supplied communication software. *Pacific Gas & Electric Company*, Sacramento, California. Programmer, 1976–1978. Supported various applications including customer activity, property accounting, and stock ownership.

Personal: Enjoy sports such as tennis and golf; playing the violin; traveling internationally.

Figure 9.3   Long Chronological Resume #1 continued

Melvin R. Smith
7210 Days Creek Road
Lexington, KY 40501
(606) 555-1234

Qualifications

As a financial executive and CPA, my areas of expertise include account-ing, systems implementation, finance, administration, computer integra-tion, computer programming, network administration, real estate development, land acquisition, construction, cash management, property management, human resources, and executive functions. I saved substan-tial amounts of money on accounting fees. I designed and/or implemented accounting, time and billing, docketing/case management, and other sys-tems. I refinanced a 200,000-square-foot shopping center, generating sev-eral million dollars.

I analyzed many properties for acquisition and prepared pro forma state-ments to obtain financing. I administered lease contracts and qualified retirement plans. I designed, installed, and administered a 50 note Novell Netware 3.11 network. I also managed major renovations, build outs, and expansions. At the personal level, I am able to sell my ideas and build con-sensus. I love problems and am a creative person, while also a sound deci-sion maker. I am able to distill information for presentation to others. I am also even tempered and tenacious.

Experience

SOUTHERN DEVELOPMENT CORPORATION   Lexington, Kentucky

CHIEF FINANCIAL OFFICER, 1997

Oversaw all financial responsibilities for a small company involved in vari-ous real estate activities, as well as over 50 related entities that were mostly individual real estate investments. The company was essentially a start-up operation relative to the real estate development side of the opera-tion. Handled all financial aspects of the company's acquisition of land and its subsequent development for manufactured housing communities. Established policies and procedures.

Implemented a new and significantly better accounting and reporting sys-tem for the company and all related entities using Timberline Gold 4.x. Organized the historical records of the company. Further, made prepara-

Figure 9.4   Long Chronological Resume #2

A A paragraph-style summary leads off this long chronological resume, which does an excellent job of documenting how Mr. Smith has contributed to each of his previous employers' bottom lines by saving money and time and improving systems and productivity.

tions to have the company become a manufactured household dealer; investigated the setting up of a joint venture with a bank or mortgage company to begin originating and servicing mortgages on the manufactured housing units that the company would sell. In addition, supported the pretrial settlement of a case for a company-related entity worth a potential of $15,000,000.

- **Consolidation of Accounting/Reporting Software:** The company was doing accounting on its various entities using different software packages, none of which were designed specifically for real estate activities. Installed Timberline Gold 4.x, and configured and set up the software for input of all entities in an integrated environment tailored to the company's business. Provided the company with a vastly superior accounting and reporting system compared to what it had previously.

- **Support of Litigation:** One of the company's related entities was involved in litigation. The books and records of the entity were in disarray. The company believed it could obtain a pretrial settlement in excess of $15,000,000. Spent two to three weeks piecing together the accounting records and history of the company to support the company in making its case for damages. Completed the necessary work to facilitate the ultimate settlement of this matter.

LOMBARD, MADISON, AND FLECK, PPLC   Lexington, Kentucky

EXECUTIVE DIRECTOR OF ADMINISTRATION, 1990–1997

Ran all of the day-to-day operations of the firm. Was responsible for all accounting and finance functions of the firm. In addition, oversaw the implementation, maintenance, and administration of the firm's computer system. Was a trustee of the firm's profit-sharing 401(k) plan. Was also chairman of the firm's executive committee, and chaired the general partnership meetings.

Personally created and installed a LAN, saving $100,000 in installation costs, and provided all necessary repairs and maintenance. Set up a computerized accounting system, a time and billing software package, and a docketing system compatible with the software. Provided secretaries with scanning technology. Took over most accounting functions from an outside CPA firm, saving $33,000 a year. Restructured the compensation formula to satisfy a maximum number of employees. Resolved merger issues,

Figure 9.4   Long Chronological Resume #2 continued

B   A problem-solution approach lets Mr. Smith dramatize his impact on each company. Each bullet describes a problem and how he solved it.

C   Throughout this resume, Mr. Smith cites figures that show how much each previous employer saved or earned as a result of his accomplishments.

saving the firm as much as $300,000 on the purchase of a branch office. Created a 401(k) plan as well.

- **Upgrade of Information Systems:** The firm was using an antiquated dedicated word processing system, and was paying a large amount annually to maintain the system. Response times for repairs were often much too slow when equipment was down. The firm's accounting system was a manual one.

The company was preparing its billing using a word processor, and this system did not give adequate information and control of attorneys' time and work-in-progress. Also, all of the posting of accounts receivable and other summaries were either manual or done via spreadsheets. Additionally, the company used an outdated docketing system for its clients' patents, trademarks, and copyrights. It also used a separate word processing-based docketing system for its litigation engagements.

- Assembly of a LAN - Determined that the firm needed a modern PC-based local area network (LAN). Vendors were making bids in the $200,000 range, more than the firm wanted to spend. Assembled the whole system myself. Within a couple of weeks had an operational network at a cost of under $100,000. Performed virtually all computer repairs, maintenance, and upgrades to the system.

- Automation of Accounting - Determined that it was necessary to implement a computerized accounting system. Investigated what was available, and selected MAS90 by State of the Art for the company's systems. Implemented general ledger, accounts payable, and payroll modules. The system was implemented, resulting in substantial time savings and improved and more timely reporting.

- Selection of Time and Billing Software - Evaluated a number of software packages, and selected TABSIII by Software Technologies, Inc. Reporting was greatly enhanced along with current data on attorney hours and work-in-progress. Centralized the billing process which resulted in a time savings to each secretary of two to four days per month of billing activity.

- Docketing System - Purchased CaseMaster III by Software Technologies, Inc., which integrated with TABSIII. It allowed the company to use a common database for client information, saving duplication of data entry, time, and potential errors. Enabled the company to integrate its intellectual property and litigation docketing systems into a single firm-wide system.

- Billing Cost Recovery - The system that was in place to bill clients for postage, copies, and faxes was very inefficient and resulted in a relatively low cost recovery rate. Found an excellent product that

Figure 9.4   Long Chronological Resume #2 continued

integrated directly with the time and billing system, virtually eliminating any manual entry. Greatly increased recovery, generating $20,000 to $30,000 of additional revenue annually.

- Document Scanning and Retention - Secretaries were retyping documents received from third parties or the firm's archives. The litigation department also needed an efficient way to retrieve documents. Acquired a scanner and optical imaging/document management software to address these issues.

■ **Accounting Cost Reduction:** Accounting costs were high for a firm of this size—in excess of $40,000 per year for quarterly compiled financial statements and tax returns. Took over most of the year-end accounting from the CPA firm, reducing its time on the preparation of the year-end statements. Also prepared internal financial statements monthly, giving the partners more information on a more timely basis. Outside accounting costs dropped to about $7,000 annually, a $33,000 savings. Tripled the reporting frequency in the process.

■ **Restructuring of Compensation:** There was growing stress between various partners based on the compensation formula that had been in place since the formation of the firm. It was obvious that a change to the formula was necessary. This task was difficult in that there would be winners and losers no matter what plan was chosen. Went through a thorough analysis over a number of weeks and had a number of meetings with the partners. Was successful in coming up with a new formula that was strong enough financially and logically to convince the partners who were negatively affected that it was equitable.

■ **Correction of a Merger Issue:** The firm had previously executed a merger agreement with a firm in Louisville, Kentucky. Became aware that there was a major defect in the agreement that would result in the firm's paying an excessive amount for the Louisville office. Discussed the issues with the managing partner and executive committee of the firm, and proposed a solution. Called a meeting of partners, which included the prior owners of the Louisville office. Appealed for an equitable solution.

Was successful in getting an amendment to the merger which resulted in an immediate savings to the firm of approximately $100,000.

Figure 9.4   Long Chronological Resume #2 continued

D This bullet shows how Mr. Smith saved money and boosted productivity for a previous employer.

E This bullet documents Mr. Smith's negotiating skills by describing his diplomatic resolution to a tricky situation that posed a real threat to the firm's future.

F Again, Mr. Smith shows how he saved a substantial sum for this employer.

Subsequently, there were other developments that would have cost the firm an additional couple hundred thousand dollars. Ultimately, saved the firm $250,000 to $300,000 in the cost of acquiring the Saginaw office.

- **401(k) Plan:** The company had a profit-sharing plan that benefited the partners and administrative staff but ignored the retirement planning needs of the nonpartner attorneys. The existing plan also fell short of maximizing what could be saved on a tax-deferred basis for all classes of employees, including the partners. Determined that the firm needed to implement a 401(k) plan. There were also certain features of the existing profit-sharing plan that needed to be preserved to protect the interests of the partners.

  Contacted a good ERISA attorney, and amended and got a favorable determination from the IRS on the existing plan, protecting the partners' interests. Then, put together the 401(k) plan and received a favorable determination on it from the IRS. Found an exceptional family of funds to offer the employees. Implemented the new 401(k) plan, and protected all of the features of the existing plan. Allowed all classes of employees to participate, and substantially provided for their future financial well-being.

SAMUEL ROSCOE ASSOCIATES, INC.   Lexington, Kentucky

CHIEF FINANCIAL OFFICER, 1986–1990

Ran the day-to-day operations of the firm, handling all of the accounting, finance, and treasury functions. Also managed the operation and maintenance of the company's headquarters, which it owned. Oversaw the firm's administrative and clerical staff of 10. Was a trustee of the firm's profit-sharing plan and 401(k) plan, which I implemented.

Obtained new accounting software for general ledger, accounts payable/receivable, billing, and payroll. Installed a Novell network, and introduced WordPerfect and AutoCad. Replaced unnecessary, $100,000 full audits with a $20,000 'review.' Created and administered formal project management systems, and compiled a database of project information. During a difficult period for the firm, handled cash management, including collections and vendor relations, and never missed a payroll.

- **Information Systems Upgrades:** At the start, all accounting and billing was done monthly and the payroll was being processed by an outside service bureau. The company was using a proprietary word processing system and had a couple PCs for spreadsheets and miscellaneous other tasks.

G

Figure 9.4   Long Chronological Resume #2 continued

G   The problem-solution approach continues as Mr. Smith describes how he successfully corrected or replaced expensive and outmoded equipment and practices.

- Accounting Automation - Recognized that the accounting systems needed to be computerized. Selected Timberline - Medallion series software, the premier accounting package for the construction/ engineering industry at that time. Implemented the general ledger, accounts payable, billing, accounts receivable, and payroll modules. Was able to speed up the accounting cycle and improve reporting. Reduced the accounting staff through attrition, saving about $70,000 annually.

- Expansion of Corporate Technology - Met with others interested in computers to discuss the latest in hardware, software, local area networks, and the advantages and disadvantages of various products. Installed a Novell network, scrapped the dedicated word processor, and brought in WordPerfect. Started using AutoCad for an ever-increasing number of drawings.

■ **Elimination of Full Audits:** The firm was having a full audit performed by a Big-8 accounting firm. It was costing the firm nearly $100,000, plus hundreds of hours expended by the staff to prepare for and assist the auditors. Upon investigation, determined that a full audit was major overkill, and all that was really needed was a 'review.' As a result, was able to reduce the outside accounting bill from $100,000 to $20,000, and greatly reduced the number of hours required to prepare for and assist the outside accountants. It saved the firm at least $100,000 per year.

■ **Project Management:** The company had no project management or job costing systems in place. It would quote a job, obtain the work, and put in hours until it was complete without regard to cost or budget. Moreover, on a regular basis the firm had to prepare proposals and quotations in response to requests for developers, governmental and quasi-governmental entities, and so on.

These activities varied dramatically in scope depending on the size of the project, its complexity, and the requirements of the prospective client's Request for Proposal (RFP) or Request for Quotation (RFQ). The firm had a lot of data about past jobs, but it was so poorly organized that it was virtually useless.

- Institution of Formal Tracking - Determined that the company needed to implement project management and job costing systems if it was to have any chance of being profitable. Implemented the systems. Provided owners and managers time lines, budgets, and timely feedback on whether or not the projects were on track. These systems did improve performance.

- Documentation of Projects - Organized the data on the historical projects, breaking down numbers of hours spent on the various phases of the projects, recording the size of the projects, the scope

Figure 9.4   Long Chronological Resume #2 continued

of the projects, and the fees earned restated in current dollars, and put all of the information in a database. This information was invaluable in responding to future RFQs and RFPs, saved large amounts of time in responding to requests, and prevented errors that could have resulted in underbidding and getting unprofitable work, or overbidding and losing work.

- **Creation of a 401(k) Plan:** The company only had a profit-sharing plan. The company's profitability was dropping off and as a result its contributions to the profit-sharing plan decreased. Employees were concerned about having enough money set aside for retirement and their children's educations. Implemented a 401(k) plan. Further, included loan provisions in the plan so employees could take out loans for the education of their children and/or other pressing needs. The plan was implemented, participation was extremely high, and employee satisfaction was greatly improved.

- **Establishment of Client Liability for Added Work:** The partners and employees of the firm would oftentimes, in their desire to serve the client and create the perfect building, do work either on their own initiative or at the request of the client that was beyond the scope of the contract, and would not bill for it. This practice was hurting the firm's profitability.

  Determined that a procedure was needed to make clients contractually liable for additional work beyond the scope of the project. Decided the company needed to raise the awareness of the employees on the scope of the contracts, emphasizing that no work be done that exceeded the scope of the contract. Instituted a policy which required a change-order that authorized the extra work be signed by the client. This change increased revenue. The policy also resulted in clients not asking for services based on their whim and fancy because now they would have to pay for them.

- **Cash Flow Management:** The firm's profitability was never very good after the death of the founder, and it was entering the end of the development cycle in the Lexington Metropolitan market. The office market was getting overbuilt, interest rates were rising, and developers were getting into financial trouble. Spent a lot of time making account collection calls, dealing with accounts payable calls, and reassuring vendors that they would get paid. Made sure the company always had the money to make the payroll. Never missed a payroll.

Figure 9.4   Long Chronological Resume #2 continued

Previous Employment

Swarthmore-Miles Company, Louisville, Kentucky - Controller/Project Manager, 1982–1985. *Cavin Transfer Incorporated*, Cincinnati, Ohio - Controller, 1980–1982. *Sablan International Forwarding, Inc.*, Cincinnati, Ohio - Director and Treasurer, 1980–1982 (concurrent and related to employment with Cavin Transfer Incorporated).

Lundby, Jones & Company, P.C., Cleveland, Ohio - CPA, Senior Accountant, 1977–1980. *Brown, McPhail and Grady*, Cleveland, Ohio - In-Charge Accountant, 1976–1977. *Ernst & Young (formerly Ernst & Whinney)*, Sandusky, Ohio - In-Charge Accountant/Staff Accountant, 1974–1976.

Education

Miami University of Ohio, Oxford, Ohio
M.B.A. 1974, Finance

University of Ohio, Athens, Ohio
B.S. 1972, Architecture

Personal

Certifications: Real Estate License - Kentucky, 1985; CPA - Ohio, 1977. Memberships: American Institute of Certified Public Accountants; Kentucky Association of Certified Public Accountants; Annual Fund Chair, Miami University Class of '74.

Figure 9.4   Long Chronological Resume #2 continued

H   Early positions, education, and personal data are briefly summarized on the last page.

A well-written long chronological resume can sell your candidacy after the interview. After seeing 10 candidates, a hiring manager may need to review resumes in order to remember specific candidates. The more accomplishments your resume includes, the better. Until you have been through an interview, you will not know what a company is looking for. If your resume includes all your major accomplishments, chances are the hiring manager will see something that hits the nail on the head.

Cover Your Entire Career

Although your resume should highlight your most recent 10 years, it must account for your entire career. Employers will be suspicious of gaps in your career and may eliminate your resume if a period seems to be unaccounted for. To make sure your entire career is included, list earlier work experience by title and company only in a section called "Other Positions" or "Additional Experience" that precedes the Education section. Hide the dates within the paragraph if you are older, so your age is not highlighted.

The Functional Resume

A functional resume stresses abilities such as purchasing, marketing, selling, managing, or analyzing. Figure 9.5 is an example of a resume organized by function rather than chronology. It can be used to gloss over a gap in your job history or frequent job hopping. If you have many skills, this kind of resume can market you as a sort of utility infielder who can perform well in several functions.

Chronology cannot be completely omitted from a functional resume. Be sure to summarize your career chronology at the bottom of the resume, as the human resource manager does in Figure 9.5.

A

Lester A. Swanson
1300 47th Avenue North, Rock Island, Illinois 64226   Telephone (555)123-4567

SUMMARY
I am a senior HUMAN RESOURCE MANAGER with a diversified background and proven track record in business, both quantitatively and qualitatively. I possess extensive experience covering a broad range of business situations, product offerings, markets, and employee involvement strategies. I am a strong LEADER, adept in CUSTOMER SATISFACTION and TOTAL QUALITY. I have created innovative solutions and made significant accomplishments in corporate, divisional, plant, and multifacility settings. *Accomplishments:*

- *EMPLOYEE RELATIONS: Successful union avoidance record, with proactive vulnerability review. **Benchmarked** an employee **attitude survey** that exceeded U.S. industry norms by 6% **overall satisfaction.** Effective discipline, behavior modification, with **no legal ramifications.** Designed and implemented **gain-sharing programs** and **suggestions systems** which have resulted in **productivity improvements** and **significant cost savings.** Implemented a salaried, nonbargaining **issue resolution** process, designed to **avoid unnecessary litigation.** Established **motivational rewards** and recognition processes.*

B

- *UNION RELATIONS: Successfully negotiated several cost-effective labor **agreements** with steelworkers, boilermakers, patternmakers, autoworkers, and the International Brotherhood of Electrical Workers without a work stoppage. Competent and proficient in **labor law,** having experience in **plant startups** as well as **closures and concession bargaining.** Handled a **decertification** with **no unfair labor practices.** Possess **a winning record of arbitration proceedings,** and overall **reduction of grievances** filed, with reduction in time and expense for resolution.*

- *SAFETY, BENEFITS, AND COMPENSATION: Reevaluated salaried positions (Hay), **saving the company from potential wage and hour violations** with exempt status. Implemented various*

Figure 9.5   Functional Resume

A Like a chronological resume, a functional resume should begin with a summary that positions the job seeker in the marketplace.

B Accomplishments are grouped by area of responsibility. Bold type draws attention to specific areas of experience, enabling potential employers to see at a glance just how diverse Mr. Swanson's talents are.

*wellness initiatives, redesigned medical benefit provisions, implemented a **preferred provider network** with employee discounts and subsequent **cost avoidance** for the company. Returned bottom-line **worker compensation reserves** with attentive management while reducing **OSHA recordables**, and implemented a comprehensive **ergonomics study**.*

■ PRODUCTIVITY IMPROVEMENT: *Redesigned **performance planning metrics** and **performance management process**, implemented **team-based award systems** for **continuous process improvement** tied to a **pay-for-performance** methodology. This process yielded median productivity improvements exceeding 30% and a **reduction in quality error rate of 34%** in a two-year period, resulting in **significant savings** and **competitive advantages**.*

EXPERIENCE

Manager of Employee/Community Relations, 1993–1998 (Salary $79,000). John Deere International, Moline, Illinois. Director of Human Resources, 1989–1993. Zonic Corp., St. Louis, Missouri. Manager of Employee Relations, 1987–1989. Schwann International, St. Louis, Missouri. Manager of Human Resources, 1986–1987. Walker Control Division, Charleston, South Carolina.

Manager of Manpower, Benefits, and Compensation, 1985–1986. Magnarom Corporation, Rockford, Illinois. Division Manager of Human Resources, 1984–1985. Advox International, Rockford, Illinois. Personnel Manager, 1979–1984. Makhoul Security Communications, Chicago, Illinois. Employment Manager/Labor Relations Administrator, 1975–1979. Randoph Company, Chicago, Illinois.

EDUCATION

MBA, DePaul University, Chicago, Illinois, 1985
BS, University of Nevada, Las Vegas, Nevada, 1974

PERSONAL

Board of Directors: United Way of Northern Illinois, Rotary, Rockford Chamber of Commerce. Member: Society of Human Resource Management.

Figure 9.5   Functional Resume continued

C Positions are listed chronologically so that Mr. Swanson's career is fully accounted for.

D Education and personal data are summarized briefly.

Make Your Resume Results-Oriented

Like a good marketer, you need to see your product—you—from your customer's point of view. Your resume needs to focus on results, not characteristics. A results-oriented resume, regardless of format, helps employers reduce the risks that are associated with hiring because they see what you have accomplished as well as your attitudes toward work.

The risks that concern employers include such matters as whether you:

- are a quality worker
- have integrity
- have excellent work habits
- can get along with others in the workplace
- may have something undesirable in your background that has created problems with previous employers

When these risks are removed, only the positives about you are left.

To reassure prospective employers, include examples of what you have done for other employers. Use your self-assessment to offer specific information about how you helped previous employers improve their profitability, recognition, and visibility. Whatever your line of work, your accomplishments in one or more of these three categories can be measured. When you provide examples, you are showing results of tests of your abilities and focusing on the needs of the employer rather than your own needs. If you have had several jobs, you should have enough material to fill several pages.

Avoid going into detail about individual goals or career objectives. If you do, the prospective employer is likely to get the impression that you are more interested in yourself than you are in the company. That can be reason enough to remove you from consideration for the job, even before a full evaluation of your credentials takes place. It is also a good idea to avoid lengthy statements about your character or the kinds of companies you worked for. Your achievements and what they meant to your past employers will be sufficient information for the reader.

What to Include

Include a description of your accomplishments for each employer, setting them out in statements that are easily read. Avoid hyperbole, but include as many facts and figures as necessary to substantiate achievements. It is important that everything included is factual. Take credit for your role in a project you managed if others were involved. Focus on past work history rather than schooling, unless you are pursuing a position in the academic, technical, or research areas where advanced training is critical to successful job performance.

If you are under 40, revealing your birth date can sell an employer on the idea that you are a go-getter with the youthful qualities of enthusiasm and eagerness. If you are over 40, however, it is better to omit your age. Someone may glance at the date and decide arbitrarily that you are too old to interview. Leaving out your birth date prevents this possibility. It allows your personal appearance to sell your youthfulness and energy.

Do Not Worry About Length

Except in the case of the short chronological resume, do not worry about the length of your resume. Instead, concern yourself with content. Ignore those who say a resume should be no more than a page or a page and a half. True, employers are busy people and they are bombarded with hundreds of resumes, especially if they have placed an advertisement soliciting resumes for a specific position. Because of this, your resume should be prepared with ease of reading in mind and should provide details that can be easily perceived by the reader.

However, that does not mean keeping your resume to a page if you have a lot more to tell the employer about yourself. You want to communicate all of your accomplishments and why you are qualified for a job. Neither your interests nor the employer's are served by the typically short resume, because it does not provide enough information for the employer to make a fair hiring decision. Most of your real competition looks just as you do on paper.

How to Use Your Resume

Just as there are many myths about what should be on a resume, there are many about how one should be used. Many individuals still believe sending a resume to an employer and then waiting for a phone call is a viable job search technique. It is not. It will just lull you into a false sense of security that you are doing something to get a job.

Resumes do not get jobs. Only interviews get jobs. At its best, the resume is a direct mail piece that has one basic purpose—to get someone interested enough to interview you person-to-person. Sending a resume to an employer and then waiting for a phone call is probably the worst way to look for a job.

You need to talk face-to-face with as many people as you can to learn about job opportunities. Take your resume with you when you go for a job interview but only give it to the interviewer if asked. If the resume does not say exactly what the employer wants to read, he or she will assume you are not the person for the job. However, if you talk to the person over the phone before seeing him or her, you may have the opportunity to revise your resume by emphasizing the points that are important to his or her company.

Talking to the employer first is always more advantageous than sending your resume blindly. Again, you do not know what the employer is looking for and most times your resume will screen you out of the process. You have a much better chance of screening your-self *in* by talking to the employer and crafting your verbal "resume" to highlight accomplishments that are most relevant to the particular interviewer's needs.

The only time to send your resume first is when you respond to a blind classified ad. Send it with a cover letter. In this instance, the cover letter becomes a selling document that has to tell the employer you are the ideal person for the job, someone who should be interviewed immediately. Give particular care and thought to its preparation, and conclude it by asking for an interview. Ideally, your resume documents the case made in the cover letter. To guide the reader to the most pertinent parts of your resume, underline or highlight the accomplishments that relate most directly to the job in question.

Finally, do not let your resume speak for you. The resume will not get you a job; only you can do that. In the end, you can sell yourself better than any resume, no matter how brilliantly it is constructed.

Part III

EXCELLING IN
THE INTERVIEW

MANY OF MY clients approach a job search believing that they know all there is to know about interviewing for a position. This is not true. If you have been out of the market for a while, the style and focus of interviewing may be quite different from what you remember. You also may be interviewing at a totally different level of responsibility, especially if you have advanced significantly over the years in your previous company.

This section will help you polish the skills you need to succeed in all kinds of interviews, so your first interview leads to the next one, and the next to the one after, until you are either hired or free to move on to the next opportunity. You will also learn how to follow up on interviews effectively and how to negotiate an attractive salary and benefit package.

Chapter 10

Preparing to Interview

THE INTERVIEW IS the most important moment of your job search campaign. In my view, it is 90 percent of the reason you get a job. That is why you simply must excel in every interview you schedule. In these critical 30 minutes, you must answer the interviewer's primary question: "Why should I hire you over other candidates who appear equally qualified?" If you can answer that question, you will give the prospective employer a reason for hiring you. However, far too many job seekers do not answer this essential question. In my experience, fully 60 percent of job search failures occur because the job seeker did not give the employer a reason for hiring him or her.

Many of these people focus only on *getting* the interview, believing they know exactly how to talk their way into a job. They think, "All I need is an interview. I can do fine after that." This conclusion is absolutely untrue. An interview is not a casual conversation. Consider the situation. The company has a job to offer, but has not yet decided to whom it will be offered. You may get the offer and you may not. Starting out, at least, all candidates are equal in the eyes of the company. The purpose of the interview from the company's point of view is to find out about you and why you should be hired over six or more equally qualified candidates. Only one person can tell the interviewer why—You!

The meter starts running as soon as you walk in. You have 30 minutes or less to make a favorable impression that extends the interview or gets you invited back for more interviews and, eventually, a job offer. To make a favorable impression, you need to know the types of questions that might be asked and how to answer each one most effectively. You need to consider the pace and order of questions and know what to delete or emphasize about yourself and your accomplishments. You need to recognize and respond to the interviewer's cues, which depend on his or her personality or interests, not yours.

In the hands of a skilled interviewer, the interview is a fact-finding, information-gathering session that is designed to ferret out specifics about you. Those specifics plus the personal impression you make are critical elements in making the hiring decision. How you handle yourself in the interview determines whether you are invited back as a finalist and ultimately get the job offer.

Types of Interviews and Their Goals

During your job search, you will participate in several kinds of interviews. Although each one is different, they all share the same goal: to help you prove on every level—social, personal, and professional—that you are distinct from and superior to other potential employees who may be equally qualified for the job. In short, each one should help you convince the employer that you are the one to hire.

This chapter and the five that follow will prepare you to succeed in four different interview settings:

• Informational or courtesy interview. In an informational or courtesy interview, there is no specific job open. You are meeting with a person to discover more information about an industry or a company or to obtain more leads that can help your job search. Frequently, this courtesy interview can be parlayed into a job offer.

• Human resources interview. In many companies the interview process begins in the human resources department. Although the human resources manager will probably not make the final decision for higher level jobs, he or she *does* have the power to recommend you to the hiring executive, the person for whom you will eventually work. An interview with an HR manager or employer should not be taken lightly. You will need to impress him or her in order to progress any further.

• First interview. A first interview has two objectives. First, you want to be liked. You want to come across as a nice, friendly person who gets along well with others. Second, you need to prove your value to the company by providing appropriate accomplishments that demonstrate your ability to make an impact. Your overall goal is to make such a good impression that you will be invited back for a second, more specific screening. The old saying, "You never get a second chance to make a good first impression," applies to the first interview.

• Second and subsequent interviews. In the second and subsequent interviews, you and the employer determine, through detailed questions and conversation about the company and its needs, whether or not you would be a good fit for the company. When both sides know more about each other and feel good about the match, an offer may be made and the conversation will turn to negotiating salary and benefits.

This chapter explains how to schedule and prepare for all types of interviews as well as how to succeed in courtesy interviews and meetings with human resources managers. Chapters 11 through 15 provide everything you need to know to stand out during your first, second, and subsequent interviews with a prospective employer.

Forget Phone Interviews

Never attempt a job interview by phone. A phone interview short-changes both you and the interviewer. You lose the opportunity to adjust your approach to the interviewer's questions by directly observing that individual, and you will never get the chance to discuss qualifications and really compete for the job. Also, the interviewer cannot elicit information as effectively.

If you tremble at the prospect of face-to-face interviews, you need to get over your fears and schedule them anyway. Use the phone to dig up information about a job in advance of an interview, but see your interviewers in person.

Advance Preparation: The Key to Success

Never be nonchalant about any kind of interview, even if you think you may not want the job. The job for which you are interviewing may not be the job that is offered. Impress the interviewer, and you may be offered a higher level position.

Approaching an interview in a casual, informal manner may put you at ease, but it may put off the employer. You need to be serious—and seriously prepared—in order to turn an interview into an employment offer. Like resumes, interviews can be used to eliminate candidates. When you are not prepared, you make it easy for the interviewer to find reasons to reject you from the running. When you are prepared, you prevent the interviewer from closing the door to a job during any stage of the negotiation.

Preparation is more than a matter of looking up an address and showing up promptly with resume in hand. It also involves investing time in listing and memorizing your accomplishments, so that when an interview is under way, you can discuss them confidently and succinctly and relate them to the needs of the company interviewing you. This kind of preparation also will distinguish you from the competition. When you are prepared, you will be able to cite your accomplishments for previous employers—accomplishments that demonstrate that you are the person this employer should hire over other competitors for the same job. When you can emphasize your past accomplishments in a factual manner, you are telling the prospective employer what you are able to do for his or her company and are setting yourself apart from all other contenders.

Preparation Does Not Mean Research

Many career experts advise job seekers to spend hours in the library investigating the companies they plan to call on. I disagree. Do not do too much homework on the company before the first interview. Your responsibility on the first interview is to listen carefully to the interviewer and answer the questions as best as you can. Many job seekers get so caught up in researching potential companies that the rest of the search suffers. You also might get the information wrong if you are trying to show off your knowledge of the company, and that will make you look foolish to the interviewer.

It is much more important to concentrate on preparing *yourself* for the interview and then committing yourself to setting up those interviews. If you make it to the second or third interview, that is when you might want to obtain additional information on the company.

Practice Makes Perfect

My firm demands a great deal from its clients. Dischargees who are under 40 are motivated to seek five to 20 interviews a week, including meetings with contacts and bona fide job interviews. Dischargees between 40 and 50 are urged to go on 10 to 15 a week; those over 50, 10 or fewer. This goal is very high. But as I have stressed throughout this book, finding a new job is a numbers game that correlates directly with the volume of interviews. If you go on 50 interviews, you will have a much better chance of winning a new job than you will if you go on only a handful of important interviews during your search.

I have said before that the more interviews you go on, the sooner you will be employed. Practice is one reason. With every interview, you become more relaxed, more at ease. You have heard all the questions and know your answers by heart. The more you interview, the more experienced and comfortable you will be with the procedures. Few new questions will take you by surprise as you learn the types of questions that interviewers ask. The element of unpredictability is largely removed and as a consequence you interview more effectively. You will also gain more confidence and self-esteem as you are invited back for a second interview, or better yet, are offered a job!

Preparing for an interview does not mean providing "boilerplate" responses to all questions. Each situation will be different and you need to adapt and mold your answers to the requirements of that situation. Chapters 11 and 12 will show you how.

Make Interviewing an All-Day, Year-Round Affair

Increase your chances of meeting a decision maker in person by:

- scheduling meetings before or after conventional business hours
- suggesting Saturday meetings when appropriate
- interviewing during holiday seasons

Schedule Interviews at All Hours of the Day

Work up a schedule of interviews for yourself and keep going. Resist the temptation to slacken or take some time off from the job search. When you do, you lose momentum, which is hard to regain. You need to establish a regular daily interview schedule.

While most of your interviews will occur between 9:00 A.M. and 5:00 P.M., interviews need not be confined to conventional work hours. Many senior managers and other decision makers have long since abandoned the eight-hour workday and are taking whatever time is necessary to get the job done. You can turn this to your advantage.

Some executives work on Saturdays. If you request a Saturday appointment, you will have the hiring executive's undivided attention, without the distraction of calls or other interviewees waiting in the wings. Asking about the availability of such an appointment also sends a positive signal to the prospective employer. Not only does it show your enthusiasm for the job, it shows your sensitivity and understanding of the interviewer's schedule and that you are willing to do whatever is necessary to accommodate it. That attitude will be appreciated.

Another option is to suggest an early breakfast interview near the office of the prospective employer. Many executives are accustomed to doing business over breakfast prior to the start of the workday.

Evening is another option. One jobless advertising executive called a Madison Avenue executive a few minutes after five one day. When that executive agreed to see him, he said, "Give me 15 minutes. I am right downstairs." The result can be an immediate job interview. Caution: seek spontaneous interviews only when you have prepared your accomplishments and are ready to answer an employer's questions. Rush into an interview opportunity ill-prepared, and your performance will suffer.

Trying to schedule interviews outside normal working hours may not work every time, but when it does succeed, you substantially increase your odds!

Do Not Stop During the Holiday Season

The holiday season can be a very productive season for interviewing. Many of your competitors will not be actively looking for jobs. They will be doing Christmas chores, going to parties, or just marking time until the first of the year. If you concentrate on arranging interviews, you may be one of the few job hunters on the street. Remember, hiring in January will be based on interviews being conducted in December.

Take advantage of the fact that potential employers have more time during the holiday season. Many will not be out of town and their schedules are lighter, unless they are in the retail business. Moreover, you may catch them in a charitable mood when they are less likely to shrug you off. Retailers probably will see you only if the need is urgent. Otherwise, they will defer a meeting until after January 1.

Do not try to reach people in the middle of the day, however. During the holiday season, these are times when hiring managers are likely to be trying to get their work done. First thing in the morning, lunchtime, and late afternoon are the best times to reach people in December.

Subtly remind the interviewer of the holiday season. An upbeat mood is always a plus in a job interview, and a warm seasonal greeting certainly helps set the tone. However, a holiday interview is not a social visit. You still must be prepared to clearly articulate exactly why and how you will benefit the prospective employer. Even during the holidays, managers do not hire people just to help them out. Concentrate on leaving the impression that you will be a great asset to the company. Do so by fitting yourself into the company's plans. Because companies are setting plans and strategies for the new calendar year, more job opportunities are available. Be sure to ask about the company's plans for the new year—and then explain how you can help achieve those goals.

Be Prompt

Plan each day's interviews the night before. Call up public transportation to confirm which train or bus to catch in order to arrive on time. If you are driving, plan your route ahead of time and factor in time for parking.

If your day includes several interviews, allow enough time to comfortably get from one interview to another. That means "back timing"—figuring out ahead how long it takes to get to a location and allowing extra time for the unexpected. All kinds of things can trap the unwary job seeker. In one case, a job seeker in a central business district who arrived in the lobby of the big office building ahead of time was still late for his interview because he did not allow enough elevator time. Beyond a certain floor, the elevators in that building stopped at every floor, causing time-consuming off-and-on traffic.

Another applicant flew into a city the evening before his interviews. He had his day all mapped out with appointments made in advance. Although he encountered no problems getting to his earliest appointment, he quickly discovered that he had scheduled too many appointments too close together, not allowing for heavy traffic. In addition, he was unfamiliar with the layout of the city. It played havoc with his interview schedule. He was on the phone apologizing for running behind all day and was unable to reschedule some of the interviews.

These are the kinds of situations you need to anticipate and allow for. It is of paramount importance to be prompt for every interview. Your promptness shows consideration for the interviewer's time and indicates that you would be a conscientious employee. Arriving late, on the other hand, makes a bad impression and may cause you to lose a job. Of course, if you do run late, call to explain and give an estimated time of arrival. The bottom line: advance planning can prevent such unfortunate events and even get you there 10 minutes early.

Dress Appropriately

Your clothes should say that you take the interview seriously. Be conservative. Bright colors, loud patterns, and clanking jewelry distract the interviewer from focusing on you. As a good rule of thumb, dress up slightly from what you would expect to wear on the job. Remember, a firm's casual dress policy applies to those who have already been hired!

Prepare for Rejection

If you interview every day for three months, you can expect to get one or two solid job offers. If you see 15 potential employers a week for those three months, you will be told "no" after 178 interviews and "yes" after just two of them.

In essence, you will be rejected until the interview that generates an offer. That is a lot of rejection to swallow, and it is hard to do alone. As Chapter 5 recommended, you need a confidante to help you process your victories and defeats. Before you begin to interview, line up a trusted friend with whom you can vent your emotions between interviews. You do not want to carry your accumulated emotions into every interview like a chip on your shoulder. Far better to express them regularly during your job search, so you can keep yourself free of resentments and fears.

While it is only natural to take all this rejection personally, you should try not to. Let me say it again: getting a job is a numbers game. You will be rejected again and again during your search. "No" does not mean that you are a valueless failure. It simply means that your accomplishments were not exactly what the company had in mind. With the help of a partner, you can maintain your belief in yourself and endure the many defeats encountered on your way to victory in the job search.

Special Advice for Salespeople

Too often, sales executives and salespeople feel that they can excel in an interview with very little preparation. These highly verbal individuals feel they can talk their way out of any situation and extricate themselves from any misstated venture. They may approach the interview as a casual conversation or ad-lib their way through the interviewer's questions. However, I find that they have the most difficulty with the interview process because they wade in too deeply and too quickly.

If you are a sales executive, restrain your natural volubility in an interview. Study Chapters 11 and 12 carefully to learn effective ways to interview, and prepare, prepare, prepare. Every word you say during an interview is important. Make sure each one is carefully considered.

Five Beliefs That Help You Succeed

Five beliefs hold the key to success or failure during interviews:

• The belief that you will make a good impression on the job interviewer. As Chapter 12 explains, the right way to make a good impression is to be whomever the interviewer wants you to be within the truthful scope of your own experience. Consciously or not, most employers tend to hire those who reflect their own views. How well you address yourself to their image of the ideal candidate will determine how much you match. Your belief in your ability to make a good impression will make this task easier.

• Confidence in your abilities. You need to convince yourself that you are the best at what you do and also get that impression across to the interviewer. While modesty usually is considered a desirable trait, it has little place in the job interview. You must tell the employer why you are wonderful without sounding like a braggart. (Chapter 11 will show you how.) If you do not tell the employer how good you are and why, chances are you will be rejected. The employer has no other way to learn what you can do except from you.

• The belief that you can show the interviewer why you are best qualified for the job. Before you even go on a job interview, you should have prepared and memorized a list of your major accomplishments so you can cite specifics when your past employment record is under discussion. When you have these facts at hand, you will be prepared to show why you are the best-qualified candidate.

• The belief that you will win the job over the competition. This requirement is closely related to confidence in your abilities. Remember, you are one of several people who are competing for the same job. All normally appear as equals to the employer, who wants to know why you should be hired over the others. Your enthusiastic, confident manner and well-prepared answers will demonstrate why.

• The belief that you will be able to prove you were the right choice for the job. Your attitude needs to say that you know you will make significant contributions once you are on the job, and the company's decision to hire you will be validated again and again. The most successful job seekers are those who have a positive attitude, and that attitude comes from knowledge that they are valuable workers who are capable of making an effective contribution.

How to Handle a Courtesy Interview

In a courtesy interview, there is no specific job open when you come in for the interview. This situation should not discourage you. If the company is one you are interested in and would like to work for, it is worth your while to attend. Make it your objective to demonstrate to the company that it should hire you. If you can come up with compelling enough reasons why you should be hired, it may happen—if not immediately, then down the road.

Follow these guidelines to succeed in a courtesy interview:

1. Begin by putting yourself mentally in the position of the employer. Think as the employer does, and you can anticipate that person's needs, formulate answers to objections that may come up, and in general identify with his or her interests. It is a way of establishing a valuable rapport.

2. Find out more about the company's plans. Most employers are willing to talk about their corporate objectives. As you listen, figure how you can fit yourself into those plans. Match your experience to what the employer is saying. If, for example, the company wants to introduce its products in new regions or territories and you have experience in launching a sales campaign, make a mental note to yourself to bring that up as a selling point.

3. Sell your primary skill first. When you have determined where you can fit in, you have several alternatives you can discuss with the employer. Concentrate first on selling one particular skill, the one you have determined may be the most important to the company based on the employer's remarks. Once you have sold the employer on that skill, you have made a major step toward being hired even though there may be no job offer or discussion of a job yet. As is true of all job interviews, the correct way to communicate your skill is to cite examples of your accomplishments for previous employers.

4. Emphasize multiple skills. Once you have sold your primary skill, marshal evidence of the other types of roles you can handle. By discussing your other capabilities, you are opening new areas. The employer perceives that you are "value added," which makes you a most attractive candidate for a future opening.

If you establish yourself as a pleasant, likeable individual, the employer may be inclined to create a job for you that did not exist when you walked in the door. At the very least, you have probably intrigued the person enough that you will be invited back for subsequent interviews or kept in mind as one of the first to be contacted when hiring begins.

After an informational interview, tell the interviewer that you appreciated him or her taking the time to meet with you. If there are no openings, ask whether he or she knows any other companies that might be hiring and whether he or she can give you contacts to see. Solicit advice about how you should proceed. These direct questions often work. More often than not people are flattered when you ask for their help and advice.

Be sure to follow up. If the employer still is in a nonhiring mode when you check back, do not assume it is a permanent situation. You can tell whether you made a good impression. If you did, it is worthwhile to keep checking back as long as there is any possibility at all of employment. If you decide it is a waste of time to call back, the employer may decide someone else should be hired.

Do not make the mistake of treating an informational interview in a casual manner. Do so, and you may lose a valuable opportunity. One job seeker set up an informational interview with a company that made it clear over the phone that it had no openings. The appointment was scheduled for 8:30 A.M. Although he planned to have plenty of time to get ready that morning, the job seeker overslept and had to rush to get ready. With no time to iron a shirt, he wore a wrinkled one. He arrived at the interview half an hour late and was told by the secretary that the person with whom he was supposed to meet was in a meeting. The individual had assumed that because the job seeker was not there on time, he was not going to show up for the interview. Later, the job seeker rationalized what had happened by telling himself that the interview did not really matter anyway because the company did not have a job opening.

You never know, however. Even if an employer tells you that there are no job openings, the situation may change. You may even miss the golden opportunity of having a job opening created for you, or at least getting the names of valuable contacts at companies that do have openings.

How to Work with a Human Resource Manager

In Chapter 7 on developing a contact strategy, I urged you to seek out the action person, the person empowered to make the decision to hire you. Unless you are in human resources, that person is not the human resource executive. That is why I recommend that you try, in some corporations, to circumvent the human resource department and try to schedule an interview directly with the hiring manager. However, that is not always possible. In many instances you will be required to begin the interview process with human resource personnel. When you are actively seeking a position at a company, you can use the human resource department to your advantage.

Human resource executives can provide many benefits in helping you get the job you want. They are excellent sources of information about the company and the job. They can help you learn where your strengths and skills may best be applied within the company, especially if it is a complex organization with many divisions and departments. The HR manager also knows what positions are available, what qualifications and experience a particular position demands, and what kind of responsibilities it entails. He or she can tell you about the company's culture, style, and the type of people who work there. This information can be a valuable measuring stick to evaluate where (or whether) you fit in that particular company and profession.

The HR manager's job is to be the clearinghouse for job openings within a company. You may approach an HR manager with one position in mind, yet end up pursuing other positions within the company. An HR executive might be aware of positions available at the company's other offices, or even at other organizations that are hiring.

When you meet with an HR executive as the first step in the interviewing process, you need to shine. The hiring executive has entrusted the HR manager with the responsibility of delivering the best candidates for a position. You must be one of the limited number of individuals selected for a second interview.

The advice an HR manager gives you at the first interview can point you in the right direction, help you focus on the right areas during your search, and give you ideas on how your experience and personal strengths can get you the job you are seeking. Take your interview very seriously, and use his or her guidance to find your way to the opportunity you are looking for.

Chapter 11

···

How to Sell Yourself with Your Accomplishments

THE HEART OF the interview is being able to sell yourself. That means using the information you uncovered in your self-assessment to develop answers that present your accomplishments without being obnoxious and provide hard facts instead of generalizations. In short, you need to brag.

If you are like most people, boasting about yourself does not come naturally. It is not easy or comfortable to tell someone all the wonderful things you have done. That is exactly what you need to do, however, when you are interviewing for a new job. If you do not tell a prospective employer how good you are, who will? In my experience, more than half of the people interviewing for jobs fail to win an offer simply because they fail to sell their accomplishments. (The other half fail because they forget to ask for the job—but more on that in Chapter 12.) More than likely you have the qualifications for the job for which you are interviewing. That should give you the confidence to tell the interviewer why your achievements make you the best person for the position.

To do the most effective job of selling yourself in an interview, you must prepare yourself in advance by compiling a list of your major job-related accomplishments. Commit the list to memory, so you are ready to elaborate on any point contained in it. You simply must be in mental command of *all* your important accomplishments. You cannot risk ad-libbing an answer to a pivotal interview request such as, "Tell me about yourself." Interviewers are after specific information, not generalities. To provide those specifics, you need to know your major accomplishments inside and out before you go into any interview.

The employer wants to discover whether you are the best person to fill the job under discussion—not only the best qualified, in the employer's view, but also the one who is oriented toward the company's goals rather than his or her personal goals. In every job interview, you need to present yourself as the best qualified person for the company's needs.

The best way to convince a prospective employer of your capabilities and your commitment is to cite what you have done for previous employers. Doing so achieves two basic objectives: you are giving the employer the information he or she needs to make a hiring decision, and you are making the most effective presentation of yourself. You are also telling him or her what you can do for that company. It is the kind of bottom-line–oriented information the employer wants to hear.

In effect, you are bragging about yourself without appearing to brag. Of course, there is a fine line between self-confidence and arrogance. To succeed in winning over an interviewer, you must learn to maximize your accomplishments and attributes without antagonizing him or her. That is the subject of this chapter.

Prepare Alternative Accomplishments

Before you schedule any interviews, sit down with your self-assessment materials, your resume, and a legal pad. Review the work history you have created and divide the examples and accomplishments you listed into various categories. Look for:

- work that resulted in cost savings
- ways you helped increase productivity
- important new business you helped secure
- projects you led successfully
- profitable ideas you developed
- anything else of bottom-line significance

Check the language you used to describe your accomplishments. Is it compelling and results-oriented? Does it clearly tell a prospective employer what you have achieved for previous employers? Revise your prose until it does.

This information must be committed to memory. During the job interview you want to be able to answer the interviewer's questions quickly and concisely. When your accomplishments are at the tip of your tongue, you will not have to sit uncomfortably while you think of your successes.

Write down multiple lists of your experience and accomplishments so you can tailor them to the company or industry where you are interviewing. Organize and reorganize this material so you have many highlights to present. Your goal is to weave them into a meaningful recitation that will hook interviewers and prospective employers. Review your lists before every interview. In fact, spend some time thinking about the industry or company and what is likely to be discussed. Make notes on what you want to stress.

Besides organizing your presentation, knowing your accomplishments will allow you to focus on hard facts rather than your own personality characteristics, such as how hard working or creative you are. In essence, your achievements will help you *illustrate* your skills instead of *boast* about them. A statement such as, "I am the greatest salesperson in the world," is clearly hyperbole. Not so the statement, "I built sales from $4 million to $20 million in just three years." That one gives the employer a solid reason to hire you!

Focus on Recent Achievements

It does not matter whether the accomplishments were achieved last week or 10 years ago—discuss them with enthusiasm! However, it is better to stress recent results rather than older ones. Mention items more than 10 years old only if they are extraordinary or are the only example of experience you possess that meets the employer's needs. When you do mention a past accomplishment, talk about it as if it happened today.

Stress Your Expertise

One of your most important interview goals is to present yourself as an expert. Many job seekers overlook this basic requirement because they do not consider themselves experts. They equate the term "expert" with a scholar who has written many volumes on a particular subject, or an award-winning research scientist who deals with abstruse information and concepts, or the individual who is at ease working with complex computers. All of these people are experts, and so are you—in your own line of work.

Your accumulated experience makes you an expert, and you must present yourself to the prospective employer in that light. Companies want experts who can acclimate themselves to the new job immediately, avoiding the time-consuming and frequently expensive trial-and-error period associated with those who lack experience.

To sell your expertise, stress:

- how you have made money for previous employers
- special assignments you have handled
- operational improvements you have instituted
- training you have conducted; people you have mentored
- speeches and presentations you have given
- your 10-, 15-, or 20-year track record in a field

"I identified the top potential major accounts in our new market and found people who could introduce me to decision makers through the back door. I set up meetings with those decision makers and brought in two major new accounts in my first six months on the job."

Demonstrate Your Ability to Get Along with Others

Getting along with others is a highly prized commodity in the workplace. Look for and list accomplishments that confirm your ability in this area. Consider:

- work teams you led or participated in
- company volunteer projects you helped spearhead
- offices and committee chairmanships you have held in professional groups, charities, or civic organizations

"I saw that members of the department were not communicating with each other. People were doing duplicate jobs and information was getting lost. I set up a series of weekly meetings where all department members could air their concerns and address problems. As a result, boundaries were clarified and rapport was increased. As communication improved, morale rose."

Highlight Problem-Solving Abilities

Examine your background for examples that showcase your problem-solving abilities. Look for:

- specific problems you solved
- improvements you were involved in
- efficiencies you were able to realize

"At Ajax, we experienced a real problem with sales executives who overspent travel budgets and could not produce receipts to back up their expense reports. I instituted a system to

monitor expense vouchers that tracked expense items that exceeded our standards and relayed information back to individuals and departments who were overspending. By monitoring and addressing those issues, I cut expenses by 18 percent."

In this era of downsized corporations, it is more important than ever to convince a potential employer that you are more interested in doing what it takes to contribute to company profits than in what the company can do for you.

Stress Outcomes and Bottom-Line Benefits

The most attention-getting accomplishments demonstrate how you can contribute to improved company profitability. Highlight ways you helped other employers improve profits. Point to specific accomplishments and try to quantify the impact on the company's or department's bottom line. Examples can include:

- a new marketing initiative that generated new revenue for the company
- a more efficient way of processing work that shortened the time by a certain percentage
- a reduction in expenses in one area of the company

"I implemented a companywide safety program that prevented lost production time by reducing job-related injuries 100 percent."

"My recommendations shortened the manufacturing cycle by two days and enabled us to reduce back orders on a profitable new product by 90 percent."

"The sales training program I planned and implemented helped our division increase sales by 82 percent in just one year."

When citing examples, use either percentages or dollar figures to indicate the magnitude of the savings or increased revenue. Also, be specific about your role in the process, whether it included creating the idea, contributing to the process, or successfully implementing the new procedures.

The old adage "time is money" is very true in today's environment. If you can point to specific examples where your work helped manufacture or deliver a product faster or eliminated steps from a process, you can quantify your contribution in terms of time saved. Potential employers can quickly translate what a savings in time will mean for their own profitability.

Making the Most of Your Accomplishments in an Interview

Remember, an interviewer's primary question is, "Why should I hire you over other candidates who appear equally qualified?" Properly presented, your accomplishments will set you apart and answer this question.

In an interview, your resume and your references will not speak for you. It is up to you to give the most convincing presentation of yourself and your abilities. This approach is terribly difficult for some people. If you have a hard time "tooting your own horn," step outside yourself and view yourself as someone else might. Rather than thinking that you are talking about yourself, pretend you are recommending a good friend.

Do not be shy about telling the prospective employer about your past on-the-job accomplishments. Let the interviewer know about everything that is germane to the position as well as the praise your work has won from your former supervisors. Make a point of mentioning any awards or honors you received in your work or a related field. If your job evaluations were consistently excellent, quote your boss's compliments.

Take as much credit as you honestly can. If you were a key figure behind a major group project, tell the interviewer. If you developed a specific idea without help, say so. If you led a project, take credit for what your subordinates accomplished under your leadership. Remember, you are there to sell yourself, not your former coworkers. You should take full credit for what you have done, but never at the expense of truth. With the current emphasis employers are placing on ethics in the workplace, stating untruths or exaggerations or including them in your resume is a sure way to remove yourself from consideration.

However, permission to discuss your accomplishments is not a license to indulge in excessive braggadocio or monopolize the interview. Avoid bombast and hyperbole, and let the interviewer do his or her job, which is to obtain information about you and evaluate how good an employee you might be. If you talk too much, he or she will never find out what you can do or make a decision in your favor.

You also need to be flexible. Although job interviews have much in common, each has its unique characteristics and should be handled accordingly. Employers today are looking for people who can contribute to the bottom line by filling specific needs. These needs vary from company to company and certainly from industry to industry. Therefore, in a job interview you must customize your remarks to the company's requirements. Giving the same responses in each interview substantially reduces your chances of being hired.

Remember, you are the seller and the interviewer is the buyer. Sell the company what it wants to buy, not what you want to sell! Listen to how the interviewer describes the company's needs and you can cite examples that prove you can help solve the company's problems and contribute to its profitability. If you concentrate only on your own agenda, you will cancel yourself out of many job opportunities.

For example, a job hunter we will call Brian started off on the right foot, but then quickly slid downhill. After writing down and memorizing a list of his past accomplishments, he went into the first interview knowing exactly what he was going to say. He picked a few examples that he felt represented his best accomplishments and decided exactly how he would present them. During the interview, the hiring manager gave several clues to the company's needs. Instead of listening carefully to what the interviewer was saying and then adapting his responses to match those needs, Brian rattled off the responses he had preselected. He was not going to be deterred from achieving his preconceived mission! He repeated the same serious mistake in subsequent interviews. He went through a month of interviews and did not receive a single call for a second interview. Because he did not respond to the employer's specific needs, other job seekers were called back instead. Inflexibility cost him the job every time.

Other individuals make the error of assuming they know exactly what the employer is looking for. For instance, an account executive named Jill scheduled five interviews in the same day, three of which were in the same industry. She wrote a list of her past accomplishments and committed the most important ones to memory. Since three of the interviews were with companies in the same industry, she decided to cite the same accomplishments in each case. Her assumption was that companies in the same industry would be looking for the same skills. In the first interview, the employer perceived the company's problem area to be the introduction of new products. In the second interview, the employer said she needed someone who could help reposition an existing product line. Company number three was adding staff to help launch a major market research initiative. In each instance, Jill recited her same prepared examples. None of them coincided with any of the companies' specific current needs.

Jill realized she needed to reevaluate her strategy. In her next interview, the hiring manager described two functional areas in which he wanted to hire someone. She listened attentively as he described these responsibilities. When her turn came to respond, she gave concrete examples that showed her ability to effectively handle the types of situations the interviewer had described. She could tell by his expression that she was on the same page as the employer. A few days later, she received a call to return for a second interview. That interview never would have occurred had she not effectively addressed the employer's specific needs.

Follow Jill's example in your interviews and be the person the company wants you to be. If you are a credit executive interviewing for a position with a company that wants to cut its bad-debt ratio, explain how you lowered bad debts in your last job by instituting a more stringent credit policy. If you are a plant manager interviewing with a company whose manufacturing is done in cells rather than in a line, talk about how you helped your last employer make the switch. If you are a marketing executive interviewing with a company that is expanding into Asia, stress your experience in supervising a team that developed and executed a marketing campaign for Asian distributors and retailers. If you never handled Asia, stress what you did in South America, so the interviewer knows you have international expertise.

As you talk, concentrate on the results of your actions without giving too many details. You do not want the interviewer to rationalize that your past accomplishments would not work at his or her company.

Sell Your Expertise When You Are Traveling Your Function

When you travel your function, you are taking your expertise outside your previous industry and finding it a new home. In these situations you need to establish yourself as an expert on your subject, although not necessarily the industry. Be sure to mention any experience you do have in the industry in question. For instance, an executive interviewing for a position as the head of public relations for a bank would be wise to mention his experience as a loan officer. By displaying an understanding of banking industry and culture, he would have a leg up on other applicants.

If there are no connections between your experience and the job you are currently seeking, try to be well informed about the industry in which you are interviewing. Read the business section of the local newspaper or study national business magazines. Acquaint yourself with the terminology and current trends within the industry. You will demonstrate your eagerness to learn and do something new—qualities every employer appreciates.

Never answer a question by saying, "I have no experience in the industry, but . . ." As Chapter 12 will underscore, you should never volunteer a shortcoming or say anything negative about yourself. Never tell an employer that you do not have something he or she wants! You cannot lie either, but you can change the subject. A financial executive whose experience is in consumer electronics could, when asked about her food industry experience, truthfully say, "All my experience has been in financial management doing cost accounting, tax accounting, and . . ." This type of response permits the executive to elaborate on her skills without mentioning the word "banking." She is trying to help the interviewer see that she is steeped in her function, an expert who can easily transfer her skills to a new field.

Never Tell the Employer How to Run His or Her Business

While it is fine to establish your expertise, it is foolhardy to tell the employer how to run his or her business. Unfortunately, this mistake is made by many so-called "industry experts" who let their egos get the best of them. When the employer mentions a problem area, the expert is right there with an instant solution, saying in effect, "Here is what you should do and how you should do it." That is the worst mistake anyone can make in a job interview. It raises a red flag and removes you as a candidate for the job. The employer knows what he or she needs and wants, and does not want to be told how to run his or her company by someone walking in the door for the first time.

Ego aside, in telling the employer how to run or change a business, you may not realize how the comments are being received. It may seem natural to apply your considerable experience to the employer's firm. Your advice may even be correct. Unfortunately, it also eliminates you from consideration.

Resist the temptation to advise when an employer tells you about a problem. Instead of offending the interviewer by bringing up an answer that may already have been rejected, talk about actual projects and achievements that are related to the issue in question. In this way you advance the merit of your candidacy without proffering the wrong answer. There is a time and place to present suggestions for improving the business, but the first interview is neither. Chapter 13 will show you how to land a job by solving a problem for an employer.

Another "industry expert" mistake is to show off your insider's knowledge about the company or the industry. The problem is that you may volunteer information that is incomplete, incorrect, or offensive to the interviewer. Of course, you should indicate that you know your industry inside out, but the best and safest way to demonstrate your knowledge is by citing your own qualifications and accomplishments.

How to Answer the Five Most Common Interview Questions

Every interview contains five basic questions that you need to be able to handle competently. In every instance, your goal is to keep doors and possibilities open. You do not want to say anything that eliminates you from the running.

What Is Your Background?

This question, which crops up in 90 percent of all interviews, can help you organize your accomplishments into a cohesive narrative. Your answer should focus on your skills and accomplishments without stressing specific job titles. If you begin with, "In my last job I served as vice president of sales," the interviewer will hear the job title and eliminate you from every other position for which you might be qualified.

Instead of supplying job titles, say (if the company wants international expertise), "I have successfully managed sales teams and am particularly strong in overseeing international sales efforts. In my last job, I expanded our global sales network from 3 to 17 countries." This answer highlights a bottom-line accomplishment instead of mentioning an attention-getting title that could distract the interviewer and shut down the interview.

Make your accomplishments as broad as possible instead of specific, and stress items that indicate your ability to get along with others. You want to keep the doors open for any opportunities within the company, not disqualify yourself at the starting gate.

The opposite is true if you are responding to a specific advertisement or opening. If you *do* want to be the vice president of sales, then it is perfectly all right to mention your previous title as well as sales milestones. However, until you know more about what kind of vice president the company is looking for, you need to play your cards close to your vest. Only careful listening will reveal whether the company wants someone who spends a lot of time in the office or stays out in the field. As these clues are revealed, your answers may become more specific.

What Do You Want to Do?

A corollary of question number one, this question is just as dangerous because it is just as specific. In the first interview, you do not want to lock yourself into a particular job. Avoid specifics and confirm your interest in the company by answering, "I want to boost sales for a company like yours."

Similarly, you should never say that you cannot do something or have no interest in something. The wrong response is, "I would like to learn more about that area." The right responses are, "I would consider it," or, "Let me tell you about something I did in a similar vein." One manager interviewed for a position with a large corporation in a department with a number of different openings. During the interview, the head of the department went through a checklist of different jobs, asking the candidate to indicate whether she had experience or interest in any of them. Practically none of the jobs named was to the candidate's liking, so she indicated no interest. She made such a negative impression on the interviewer that she was not offered a job.

What Don't You Do Well?

Encountered in about 15 percent of all interviews, this question tempts you to volunteer your shortcomings—something you should never do in an interview. It is closely related to the classic question, "What are your strengths and weaknesses?"

As Chapter 12 will emphasize, you need not provide a full answer to these questions. Everything you do or say in an interview should be positive. As far as you are concerned, there are no negatives. You cannot convince an employer that you are wonderful by talking about what you do not do well. If you are pressed for an answer, one response might be, "I like to work with other people. I would not do well shut off in an ivory tower somewhere." This answer confirms your ability to get along well with others, a far more important ingredient in job success than most technical skills.

What Kind of Money Do You Want?

If possible, money should not be discussed in the first or second interview. The longer you can talk without discussing income or benefits, the better off you will be, because you want to strengthen the relationship between you and the company before pinning down a salary. However, if you are asked directly, you will have to give a truthful answer. If you made $50,000 on your last job, do not say you made $75,000. Your previous salary is your value, and you gain nothing from dissembling. Chapters 12 and 15 offer pointers on negotiating salary.

Why Did You Leave Your Last Position?

In my view, this query is *the* most dangerous question you will encounter. For anyone who has been discharged, this question is a minefield. In fact, Challenger, Gray & Christmas counselors can spend hours helping clients find an answer to this question.

You need to develop an answer that is short, succinct, and true. It cannot say anything bad about you or a previous employer. It is natural to want to lay blame for your departure on someone else, but you cannot. Your goal is to develop one answer that works and then stick to it. Changing your story from interview to interview will make it hard to remember what you said at which appointment, and eventually the discrepancies will catch up with you.

This question is easy to answer if you were part of a very large downsizing. "A thousand of us left when the company was purchased by Xydeco last fall," is a simple, truthful, and nonblaming reply. "I did not get along well with my colleagues," and "I did not get along well with my boss," are disastrous answers. The interviewer will presume you cannot get along with his or her colleagues either.

Although the answer you formulate must be true, it does not necessarily have to be the real reason you left your company. A good example is, "I was blocked. There was no place to go in the company." Everybody knows people who cannot move up because higher level jobs are filled by people their own age, and the interviewer will sympathize without questioning you further. Another possibility is, "I was on the wrong team. A new group came in and wanted its own people." These answers must be truthful even if they are not germane.

Spend time developing a statement that is innocuous and very short. The more you talk, the less the interviewer will believe. Keep your answer short and simple, then change the topic.

Chapter 12

Do's and Don'ts of the First Interview

EVERYTHING YOU DO when you are looking for a new job should be directed toward one central goal: getting the job offer. You may decide not to accept the offer, but you still have to receive it before you can make that decision. You must do everything you can within moral bounds to get a job offer, and then evaluate it. Do not be overly concerned about the job itself at the beginning of the interview. Get the offer and then decide whether you want it.

To obtain an offer, you need to demonstrate that you are the person the interviewer wants you to be. After all, you are a product. You need to be the product the buyer wants to buy, not what you, the seller, wants to sell! Qualifications and accomplishments are not the only prerequisites for getting a job. Ultimately, you will be hired because the interviewer likes you the best, not necessarily because you are the most qualified in the field of candidates. The more you are like "me" (i.e., the interviewer), the better you must be.

This chapter explains how to listen for clues about what the company is looking for as well as how to tailor your answers to fit that image. It will show you how to showcase the scope of your skills, desires, and talents so that you will be invited back for additional discussion.

Do's and Don'ts of the First Interview

Do . . .

- make a good impression
- smile
- let the interviewer set the agenda
- think first of the company, not your own needs
- listen carefully
- keep questions to a minimum
- tell the truth
- watch your body language
- make eye contact
- build rapport with the interviewer
- offer references
- ask for the job!

Don't . . .

- volunteer shortcomings
- criticize former employers
- talk too much
- play hard to get
- tell jokes
- talk about money

What You Should Do in a First Interview

Make a Good First Impression

First impressions are vital. If you do not make a good impression immediately, the chances are that you will not be able to recover, however excellent your qualifications. Studies indicate that the majority of interviewers will eliminate you in the first 10 minutes. You do not want to be rejected out of hand. If you do make a mistake or present yourself in an unfavorable manner in the interviewer's opinion, you have erased your likeability factor. Your likeability factor is important. People buy self-images. They think, "The more you are like me, the better you must be." If your first impression convinces the interviewer that the two of you are similar, he or she will be more receptive to you.

When you walk in the door, the interviewer is sizing you up and registering that all-important first impression. If you appear to be relaxed, confident, and natural, you are on your way to making a good impression in the first five minutes.

Look the interviewer directly in the eye and smile when you meet, using a firm but not hard handshake. These initial gestures are important. If you avert your gaze, you may seem shifty or unsure of yourself. If you give the person a "wet fish" handshake instead of a solid one, you may seem timid and ineffectual. If you crush the interviewer's hand, the pain will dim your luster.

Always try to be "up" psychologically for the interview. That is often difficult, especially if you have been job hunting for some time. However, it is very important for the success of your interview. If you appear downcast or depressed, or are unresponsive to the interviewer's questions or listless in your approach, you will rule yourself out of consideration for that job. Interviewers want enthusiastic, happy people who show a strong interest in the job. If you do not, another candidate most assuredly will.

Part of making a good first impression is being a good guest. Respond to the interviewer's hospitality. Accept anything that is offered. If you are offered but do not drink coffee, take a sip or two and then just leave the cup. The interviewer is your host; you are the gracious guest.

If you are a smoker, by all means do not light up. If the interviewer wants to smoke, it is his or her prerogative. You should avoid it, unless you are offered a cigarette.

A good guest also can accept a compliment. If the interviewer compliments you on an accomplishment (quite likely, since they are the subject of the meeting), accept it gracefully. A job interview is no place for self-deprecation. There is only one appropriate response to a compliment: a thank you with a smile.

During your visit, treat everyone with the utmost courtesy and respect. Do not do anything that will permit the employer to take offense and not want to help you in your job search.

Smile, Smile, Smile

You will find it very difficult to connect with your interviewer if you enter the room wearing a frown or a worried scowl. Show your confidence by smiling and acting upbeat. Companies hire people they like! A smile sets the tone for the entire session, projecting you as a pleasant person.

Job hunters who have been discouraged by a past job dismissal sometimes wear their emotions on their sleeves, acting defeated before they even begin. Interviewers sense this kind of negativity and the job applicant's attitude becomes a self-fulfilling prophecy. A warm smile and a congenial, friendly attitude help set the tone of the interview and show that you have the kind of social skills necessary to work with others.

Let the Interviewer Set the Agenda

Your potential employer has a limited amount of time and will talk about what is important to him or her. Therefore, be nondirective. Allow the interviewer to choose exactly what to discuss. With only 20 to 30 minutes available for the conversation, you have no time to interject an agenda of your own or discuss points you think should be covered. Doing so is an invitation to an early exit.

Careful listening will reveal the interviewer's agenda. Listen for clues as to what he or she wants. Anticipate the interviewer's questions as much as possible. If you have memorized your list of accomplishments, you should have no trouble customizing your remarks to the company's—and the interviewer's—requirements.

Again, you are in the role of the seller and the interviewer is the buyer. Make sure you listen to what the interviewer is saying when he or she describes the company's needs. Respond by citing examples of your work that prove you can help solve the company's problems and contribute to its profitability. If you concentrate only on your own agenda, you will cancel yourself out of many job opportunities.

Think First of the Company, Not Your Own Needs

It is only natural to view a company or a job in the context of your own interests and objectives first. After all, you have to choose a place where you feel you can be happy and one that will meet your needs. However, during an interview you need to downplay your own needs and give top priority to the needs of the company. Employers are not primarily interested in your goals. They want to know what you have done and what you can do for them. Therefore, never say that a position will be a good career advancement or a learning experience. Not only are you telling the employer that you are more concerned about yourself than the company or the job, but you are asking the employer to turn his or her company into a testing ground for your capabilities so you can move on to the next employer at more money! No one wants a learner. The corporation wants someone to improve profits, sales, or operations now.

Instead of discussing your own goals, listen to what the interviewer has to say. When you know what the company is looking for, you can use the proper facets of your background to convince the interviewer that you are not only the best-qualified person but also the one who is oriented toward the company's goals rather than your own personal objectives.

Listen Carefully

Many people are understandably nervous during a first interview. They are so eager to say the right thing that they often do not listen carefully. They begin to answer a question (at least in their minds) before the interviewer has finished asking it. However, you cannot talk yourself into a job. You need to listen, too. Being a good listener means making eye contact with the interviewer and showing a genuine interest in what he or she is saying. Let the interview unfold at a relaxed place—but remember, this talk is no casual conversation. It is possibly your whole future. Let the interviewer tell you what he or she is looking for. Listen for clues and respond in a manner that confirms that you understand the company's needs and can meet those requirements.

A marketing executive who listened well and asked appropriate questions during an interview learned that the firm was planning to open a branch office near her home. She expressed an interest in working there and consequently found a job that was a much easier commute than the one she originally sought.

Interviewers appreciate and often reward the kind of thoughtful interview that comes only from paying attention and listening well.

Keep Questions to a Minimum

Most people think that asking questions during an interview makes them appear intelligent. Unfortunately, questions may lose more positions than they gain. Keep questions to a bare minimum. It is the company's job to find out about you and why you should be hired; it is also the company's prerogative to ask questions. Your job is to answer the questions and also do a lot of listening. If you talk longer than 15 minutes out of each hour, you will endanger yourself by saying or asking something that may turn off the person across the desk.

Asking numerous questions, especially in an attempt to show off your knowledge about the company, may make the interviewer feel uncomfortable and on the spot. Perhaps the interviewer cannot answer your question or feels you are prying into company secrets. Your question may even touch on a sore point. A simple question like, "How is your new product line doing, the one you introduced at the Alpha Trade Show last spring?" may offend an interviewer who objected to the line and was outvoted, or supported it and is now in hot water due to low sales. He or she may not be interested in giving you an answer you might eventually take to the competition. Without ever knowing why, you may be eliminated as a candidate for the job. Play it safe and do not show off by asking unnecessary questions.

Many of your questions about the company may be legitimate. Keep in mind that all your questions eventually will be answered if the company decides it likes you and makes a job offer. If the company decides it does not like you, your questions do not make any difference. You will not get the job offer under any circumstances. Postpone questions about the company until the second or the third interview. Better yet, ask them *after* you get the offer. There will be plenty of time for questions and answers as you negotiate the offer.

Tell the Truth

It is absolutely essential not to lie or exaggerate. However, you can puff. Unfortunately, too many people exaggerate when pressed for information on past responsibilities, skill levels, and other pertinent details. Often, exaggerations turn into lies. For example, if a store manager tries to pass himself off as director of more than one store, he also has to lie about his responsibilities and salary level. When an aspiring executive lies about his education, he also has to fabricate his skills and abilities. One lie leads to another and soon the situation becomes a house of cards—one false move and everything comes crashing down. If the interview does result in a job offer, the lies almost always come back to haunt the new employee. Deceit quickly destroys the atmosphere of trust that is so vital to a good employee-employer relationship.

Role playing also has no place in the interview. As a job seeker, you want to perform well on the basis of fact, not fiction. If you obtain a position because you have played a role, the job will disappear once you tire of playing that role—or when it becomes clear that you do not have the right background to hold the position. Do not exaggerate your education, pretend to be a world traveler, or claim to know celebrities or influential people if in fact you do not. Even if you do, there is no reason to discuss those relationships in an interview! Name-dropping can be negative, unless you are dropping the names of potential customers you can legitimately bring to the company.

Be yourself in every interview. When you examine your skills and accomplishments, you will find that there is no real reason why you cannot win a new job based on what you realistically have to offer, rather than on some fictitious creation of yourself.

You also need to be truthful about problems you may have encountered previously. Do not discuss anything unpleasant in your background. It is best to deal with it honestly or try to avoid the subject by "misinterpreting" the question and saying something that is true that sounds like a response. Then try to move on by mentioning something more upbeat. Never give the company a reason not to hire you.

Watch Your Body Language

Some of the most important communication in job interviews has nothing to do with words, written or spoken. It has to do with your body language. It is true that our bodies betray our inner feelings. The right kind of body language can boost your odds of getting the offer. The wrong kind of body language can sabotage your chances.

Most adverse body language is the result of tension or nervousness. Nerves can cause some spectacular mistakes! I knew one individual who was so flustered at the prospect of the interview that he accidentally knocked over the chair he was going to sit in. Another attempted to smoke and accidentally stubbed her cigarette out on the interviewer's desk. She missed the ashtray. Gaffes of this sort are difficult to overcome in the job interview.

You are good. There is no need to be nervous, but a little tension will start the adrenalin flowing and make you a better interviewee. Too much tension, however, can be counterproductive. Concentrate on the interviewer and you will have less time to grow nervous thinking about yourself. Your attention will also make the interviewer feel witty, charming, and urbane. The better the interviewer feels, the better you will feel, and the more likely you will make a favorable impression. The more attention you focus on the interviewer, the more you will relax and the less you will have to be concerned about unfavorable body language.

When you seat yourself, assume a comfortable posture and keep your body still. Avoid fidgeting, shifting your position, or crossing and recrossing your legs, since it may give the interviewer a message that you are uneasy, nervous, or trying to conceal something.

If you cover your mouth as you answer a question, you are suggesting that you are uncomfortable or unsure about the statement you are making. If you cross your arms or legs during the interview, you are shutting the interviewer out—the last thing you want to do!

If you slouch in your chair, you imply that you do not care enough about the company to be careful about the impression you are making. Drumming your fingers, flexing your feet, examining objects on the interviewer's desk, or fixing your gaze out the window are all irritating and distracting to the interviewer. Do not try to make a dramatic impression by pacing back and forth with hands clasped behind your back! None of this advances your job prospects and more likely than not will damage them.

Another type of negative body language is "freezing" in the interview—sitting very erect, not moving a muscle, and answering questions in a virtually expressionless manner. The interviewer may conclude that you are too withdrawn to make a good employee. Freezing may be your personal defense against stress, but it prevents the interviewer from getting to know the real you.

To find out whether you are expressing negative body language unconsciously, ask a trusted friend or confidante to participate in a simulated interview. If you have been interviewing, you know the kinds of questions interviewers ask. With few exceptions they do not vary greatly from interview to interview. After a few interviews it is unlikely that you will hear a "new" query, although the words and phrasing may be altered. Select the toughest and most representative questions and have your friend interview you. Ask him or her to observe you as you answer. Afterward, the two of you can critique your physical reactions. Through this process, one job seeker discovered that he was tapping his foot constantly on the floor and took immediate steps to end this nervous tic.

Another way you can help yourself is by avoiding stress-building situations. Give yourself plenty of time to reach the job interview site. Do not be late or so close to the appointment that you are racing the clock. Arriving at the interview out of breath or with a feeling of apprehension because you are a few minutes late is bound to be reflected in the job interview. Your bottled-up tensions will be revealed by your body language.

Also, try not to handicap yourself with personal or emotional problems. Put them aside for the duration of the job interview. No one wants to hear negatives in your personal life. Concentrate on the interview so you do not appear nervous or flustered. It may take some emotional discipline, but you must do it.

Body Language to Avoid

Take steps to eliminate these mannerisms, which are irritating, distracting, and send the wrong message about you:

- bobbing knees
- tapping or drumming fingers
- covering your mouth
- flexing your feet
- invading interviewer's territory

- examining objects on the interviewer's desk
- slumped shoulders
- averted gaze
- crossed arms and legs
- staring out a window

- fluttering hands
- poor posture
- slouching
- pacing
- tapping feet or toes
- closing eyes while thinking

Make Eye Contact

While our culture considers it impolite to stare, most interviewers will wonder what is wrong if you are unable to hold their gaze. Looking every which way but at the interviewer conveys the impression that you are hiding something or are unsure of yourself. In general, powerful people make more eye contact than those who are less confident. Follow their lead and make it a point to look at the interviewer directly when you answer questions. Frankly, I believe there is no such thing as too much eye contact in an interview. In my view, the more eye contact you can make, the better.

Build Rapport with the Interviewer

Rapport sounds elusive but is actually quite simple. It means giving the interviewer what he or she wants. Remember, employers want to hire people they like—people with complementary skills and personality traits who will fit in well with their new team. To build rapport with the interviewer, subtly underscore these similarities.

You cannot underscore similarities until you have established them, however. Unless you know the interviewer's personal interests, attempting to establish a relationship with him or her based on personal interests may be treading on dangerous ground. You do not know what is on the interviewer's mind or that person's taste or preferences. If, on a bright day, you tell that person, "It certainly would be a fine day to be on the ski slopes," your wish may be granted quickly if he or she is not interested in skiing and thinks you are more interested in skiing than working.

On the other hand, if the interviewer's desk has a picture of a family member gliding down a ski slope, your statement or a similar question could well be an opener to start building rapport. Similarly, if you are asked, "Do you think the Celtics will do well this season?" do not reply by saying you do not like basketball! Even if you do not like basketball, do not volunteer the fact or you may not get the job. Keep your dislike to yourself, and you have a fighting chance.

When you can establish that you and the interviewer have something in common, your mutual interest can be instrumental in winning a job. Take advantage of any common interest that surfaces. One senior level executive who had written a handbook on sailing happened to talk to a prospective employer who was a sailing enthusiast. This client actually got a $150,000 job that did not exist when he walked in the door.

Positive personal information also can build rapport and transform a routine question-and-answer session into a friendlier discussion. For instance, if you say that you have five children, the interviewer may nod knowingly and say, "Yes, I have a large family, too." Immediately, a common bond is acknowledged and the interviewer sees the candidate in a more sympathetic and caring light.

Remember, people hire people they like and with whom they share some common ground. The connection between you and the hiring authority can be strengthened when you volunteer personal information. While antidiscrimination laws bar the interviewer from asking about your marital status and age, you can volunteer any-thing you feel will help get a job offer.

Offer References

Few employers actually check references, except for lower level posi-tions. In our litigious society, former employers tend to confirm only the length of your employment, your salary, and your title. Prospec-tive employers know that you will not be given a bad reference, so they look elsewhere to confirm that you are who you say you are. Quite likely they will use the corporate grapevine to find someone in your former company who can fill them in.

Still, you need to be prepared to name a reference when you are asked. I recommend recruiting 15 people to serve as references. You can use each one a maximum of three times before he or she grows tired of responding to a company's questions. Save your best refer-ences for your most important interviews.

If you were discharged from your previous employer, ask a friendly former colleague at an equal level to act as a reference. If you reported to the president and the president does not like you, ask another vice president or executive. Do not name your former boss unless you were downsized.

In general, I have found that former bosses make poor refer-ences. If the person let you go, he or she will feel compelled to jus-tify that decision and will probably say something negative about you. Even if it is not true, the damage will be done. The hiring com-pany will buy his or her perception.

Ask for the Order!

Many job seekers impress the interviewer with their personalities and qualifications but do not win the job offer simply because they do not ask for it! They do not say they are interested in the job or give the employer a reason to hire them. They want the employer to chase them. Faced by a seeming lack of enthusiasm, the employer concludes that the person is not interested and dismisses him or her from consideration.

You must give strong clues that this is the job for you. At the end of the interview, come right out and say, "I can do this job. Will you hire me?" or "When would you like me to start?" In sales parlance, you must ask for the order. Nothing less will impress the employer. There is no reason to hesitate. Your eagerness will not compromise your bargaining position. In fact, if you show no enthusiasm—you will have no bargaining position at all! The employer will appreciate your aggressiveness and will interpret it as a sign of interest and enthusiasm, qualities all employers want. "If you like me and my company, I will like you better."

When you ask for the order, be sure to clarify your next step. You will probably hear the classic line, "Don't call us; we'll call you." Ignore it, and follow up with a letter or a phone call a week later. (See Chapter 14 for the most effective ways to follow up after an interview.)

Do's and Don'ts for Workers Over 50

During the interview . . .

• **DO stress past examples of loyalty to your former companies** to demonstrate your unwillingness to jump ship at the first available opportunity. Although ongoing layoffs have severely tested employee/employer loyalty, employers still need to feel that employees are 100 percent committed to the company.

• **DO emphasize relevant experience** that tells the prospective employer you will not have any kind of learning curve. It is important to convince the interviewer that you can do the job now!

• **DO mention work experience that demonstrates your flexibility and creativity** to counteract stereotypes that suggest those over 50 do not have imagination. Discuss ways you solved problems and developed ideas to make your former employer more profitable or more competitive.

- **DO look and act young.** Everyone knows 50-year-olds who look and act as if they are 65 and 65-year-olds who look and act as if they are 50. Dress in fashionable clothes and show enthusiasm for your work. Exhibit a sense of excitement and energy, traits that younger individuals do not always show.

- **DO emphasize your knowledge of current technology.** You do not want to appear as if the world has passed you by. Let the employer know which software programs you know and which things you are comfortable doing.

- **DON'T apologize or act defensive about being over 50.** Never say, "Nobody really wants to hire someone who is over 50." A defeatist attitude will show during the interview. Employers want to hire people who are confident in themselves and their abilities, regardless of age.

- **DON'T lead with your resume.** It might show that you graduated from college before your interviewer was born! Use the interview to sell your experience and what you can offer the company. Leave your resume with the interviewer at the meeting's conclusion if asked but do not offer it before the interview begins unless you are specifically requested to do so.

- **DON'T mention retirement.** It reminds interviewers that you are older and implies that retirement is more important to you than the job. Strike the word "retirement" from your vocabulary.

- **DON'T mention accomplishments you made more than 10 years ago** unless they are extraordinary or the only example of experience you possess that meets the employer's needs. If you do mention a past accomplishment, talk about it as if it happened today.

- **DON'T talk down to, patronize, or become convinced that you could not work for a younger manager.** You do not want to make the interviewer feel that you are superior to him or her. If you have a problem working for someone younger than yourself, resolve this conflict immediately because odds are you will work for people younger than you. It is a reality you have to accept and deal with properly.

- **DON'T discuss events or happenings of many years ago**, no matter how fresh and recent they seem to you. They may not seem fresh or recent to a younger interviewer. When you focus on long-ago events, you give the impression that you are focused on the past rather than the future, and that is enough to remove you from the competition. Employers want forward-looking, not backward-looking people.

What You Should Not Do in a First Interview

Do Not Volunteer Your Shortcomings

Never say anything negative about yourself in an interview. Your primary task is to tell the prospective employer about your positives. If you raise any negative matters, you are only imposing handicaps on yourself, making it that much harder or even impossible to succeed in the job interview.

A common land mine is to volunteer personal shortcomings in response to the question, "What are your strengths and weaknesses?" Although this question is a cliché, it is still used often. Respond to this question by sticking with your strengths and avoiding the weaknesses. You should never volunteer what you do not do well! Even a statement that appears harmless, such as, "I am impatient with inefficiency," is dangerous. It may be interpreted as a sign that you have a quick temper, are hard on subordinates, or cannot handle a difficult situation without losing control. Turn the "weakness" part of the question around to achieve a positive advantage for yourself.

Here is another example of the *wrong* way to respond to the question, "What don't you do well?"

"It takes me time to get accustomed to new situations or routines. I work to my fullest potential on assignments with which I have some familiarity."

Although you have explained how you work best and have not said anything that implies you are incompetent, this response proves that you will have a problem adjusting to a new situation. That is not the message you want to send the interviewer. A better answer is,

"I really like to be challenged. I would be frustrated if I were in a situation that did not use my abilities."

Many individuals who question you about strengths and weaknesses are not experienced interviewers. (In fact, most executives are not experienced interviewers unless their background is in personnel.) It gives you the opportunity to take command of the situation by rendering information about yourself that you want presented and emphasizing the points concerning your accomplishments that you want emphasized. Although the interview should not become a monologue on your part, you should be able to steer the conversation in the direction you wish it to go.

Remember that the interviewer wants to know why he or she should hire you. How are you better than the other candidates who are applying for the same job? That is the unspoken question in the interviewer's mind. Respond with a set of positive reasons that answer the question without clouding the issue with negatives. The degree of your success will indicate whether or not you get the job offer.

Do Not Criticize Former Employers

It is never a good idea to criticize former employers or superiors in an interview. When you criticize your old boss, the new employer will think you are a complainer. Who wants to hire a person with a chip on his or her shoulder?

It is tempting to criticize former employers to salve your ego, especially if you happen to harbor some animosity toward one or more of them. It seems like an ideal opportunity to "get back" at someone who you think treated you unfairly. You may have excellent reasons for criticizing a former employer. Nevertheless, forget it.

Keep your negative thoughts about former employers to yourself. Give the impression that as far as you are concerned, everyone you ever met was nice. Search for positives about your relationships with former employers, and by all means be positive in discussing your work and your contributions to these corporations. If the interviewer asks a question such as, "What didn't you like about your former job?" avoid a negative response and concentrate instead on the favorable aspects.

Even more important, avoid giving the impression that you had problems with people. Remember, employers want to hire applicants who can get along with others. Indicate that there has been friction, dissent, or outright conflict in some of your past associations, and you lessen or even eliminate your prospects of landing the job, no matter how spectacular your abilities and qualifications. For example, a former executive in the graphic arts industry called a prospective employer to arrange for an interview. The employer seemed pleased by the job candidate's background and agreed to meet. During the interview, the former executive was asked why he would make an effective manager. Instead of citing specific examples of effective management from former jobs, he described multiple bad experiences with former employers, said he learned from their mistakes, and knew he would do a better job than any of them had. At the conclusion of the interview, the prospective employer wished the job candidate good luck. Upon reviewing the interview later, the executive realized he had made a grave mistake by talking so negatively about his former employers. He did not receive a job offer.

Do Not Talk Too Much

While modesty has no place in the job interview, talking *too* much *can* ruin an interview and your chances for the job. To an interviewer, the person who talks too much in a job interview may show bad judgment. You may project yourself as a know-it-all who is more concerned with your own needs than the company's. Worse, you may appear to be someone who shoots from the hip or speaks without thinking—something few companies can afford in today's highly competitive global market. No one ever lost a job by keeping his or her mouth shut, but many jobs have been lost by talking too often and too long! As previously stated, it is impossible to monopolize a conversation without saying something that rubs the interviewer the wrong way.

Do not talk more than is absolutely necessary. Listen for clues as to what the interviewer is looking for, and adapt your responses to what is needed. If a company wants an advertising executive, it does no good to tell them how good you are in product development. Instead of letting your ego get in your way, be friendly and respond in a manner that matches the attitude of the interviewer.

Do Not Play Hard to Get

Do not communicate to the hiring executive that the company needs to convince you that the opportunity would be a good career move, or that you might be interested in the job if certain conditions and advance guarantees are met. This approach is almost always disastrous, yet many job seekers approach their search this way.

Playing hard to get is never successful. Employers are interested in what you can do for them, not what you expect them to do for you. When you start dictating terms, you send the message that you are more concerned about self-interest than you are in the job, and that will immediately turn most employers off.

Do Not Tell Jokes

Do not try to appeal to employers through their sense of humor; the job interview is no place to tell jokes. In fact, one of the worst ways to start an interview is to try to make a joke about something the interviewer says and follow that up with laughter. You may have just joked yourself out of the running for that job!

Do Not Talk About Money

Questions regarding salary and benefits may be at the top of your mind when you apply for a job, but they are not the employer's main concern. If you can, avoid mentioning money, benefits, and related matters in the first interview. To many hiring executives, doing so is like waving a red flag. It implies that you are more interested in yourself, whereas the hiring executive is interested in what you can do for the company—how you can add value and profitability to the organization.

Once the company decides it likes you and wants to make an offer, enough information has been exchanged and proper rapport achieved to embark upon the delicate issue of money. In reality, the longer you talk, the more likely the salary proffered will increase. Do not sabotage your chances by discussing monetary needs before the potential employer has a chance to understand your qualifications and feel comfortable with the match between the company's needs and your background. Resist attempts to discuss money and keep the employer focused on your capabilities and accomplishments where the spotlight belongs.

Chapter 13

Do's and Don'ts of the Second Interview

THE BOTTOM LINE in job search success is being liked in the interview. When you are liked in the first interview, you may be asked to return for successive interviews. You have already made your first impression; now you need to continue to distinguish yourself from other contenders through your accomplishments and your personality. Basically, the recipe for success in second and subsequent interviews is: do more of the same, and do it better.

Do's and Don'ts of the Second Interview

Do . . .

- polish your answers
- be patient
- begin to research the company
- provide solutions when asked

Don't . . .

- discuss salary and benefits until the interviewer raises the subject

What You Should Do During the Second (or Third) Interview

During subsequent interviews, you and the prospective employer will continue to get to know one another. Through questions and discussion, you will gain a better grasp of the company's needs while the company develops a clearer picture of who you are and what you can do. Follow these guidelines to make a strong finish and secure a job offer.

Polish Your Answers

The questions you will encounter will be identical or similar to the questions in the first interview. As before, questions contain clues. When someone asks, "Are you creative?" you can assume that the company values creativity and wants a creative person to fill the job. If you hear, "How do you feel about overseas travel?" you can bet that a passport comes with the position.

Do not answer any question with a simple yes or no. Use your accomplishments to explain why you are creative or why you are comfortable traveling overseas:

"I was the person who conceived and designed the propeller that doubled the speed of the XL44 jet ski."

"When I supervised the marketing activities of dealers in 10 countries, I was on the road about half the time."

After dozens of first interviews, you have your answers to the five most common interview questions down pat. You will hear these questions again and again in subsequent interviews. Answer them patiently, and always with your accomplishments. Two new questions you may encounter are: "What do you want to be doing in five years?" and "Do you like the sound of this job?" Answer with a description of the job plus the words "with your company" or "working for you." By the second or third interview, you have gleaned enough information about a company's needs to start answering questions like these more specifically. Although your answers need not be as broad as before, it is still a good idea to focus on accomplishments rather than previous job titles. Continue to sell your ability to get along with others just as heavily as you peddle your skills and accomplishments.

Be Patient

Second interviews cover much of the same ground as the first, but in greater detail. However, no matter how many times you have already responded to a question, it is your job to respond again as graciously and enthusiastically as you did the first time.

Above all, do not betray any impatience with the process, or indicate that you have already answered a question or discussed an issue. I recall one manager who applied for a job at a branch location of a company, made a good impression on the head of the office, and was invited to interview at the firm's headquarters in another city. He spent most of the day being interviewed by various people there and touring the company's facilities. At one point he was asked to revisit an area where he had been earlier in the day. His reply was, "I have already seen that." He could tell by the red flush on his host's face that he had erred. Although he was treated courteously for the remainder of his time there, he sensed that he had made a serious mistake from which he would not be able to recover. What difference would it make if the employer showed him the same area four times? The employer felt it was important, and that is all that counts. The candidate has no license to shut off the employer, as this man did. When the manager arrived back at his home city and checked with the head of the local office, the company no longer had any interest in hiring him. Small wonder; he had blown a good opportunity.

The company holds all the cards, and it can do what it wants. Let the company win. If the job or people are awful, you can always reject an offer.

Begin to Research the Company

In my view, it is not important to research a company before a first interview. In the first interview, it is better to listen to what the company has to say about its needs than to come in with preconceived notions of what it is looking for. By the second or third interview, research has a place.

Check the library for information on companies that have offered you a second interview. You may begin to be questioned about your knowledge of the industry and where that company fits in. While you should not waste your time memorizing the annual report, knowing basic information about the organization will make you more impressive in later interviews. In some cases, the HR executive can help you fill in the details about the company.

You also might want to make sure that the company is not about to be acquired or folded into another company. Although there is opportunity in chaos, I think it is foolhardy to accept a job in a department that may be eliminated in a merger. You will not have time to establish your value to the employer and you will be a prime candidate for the "last hired, first fired" scenario.

When Asked, Provide Solutions

It is never appropriate to tell an employer how to run his or her business. However, under certain circumstances, you can prove your value to an employer by tactfully and creatively providing a solution to a problem.

Often during the course of an interview, an employer may talk about the company and mention a particular problem or an area they would like to expand or develop new ideas for. If this happens, you have just been handed a golden opportunity. Whether or not the employer asks for it, volunteer to help solve the problem. Even if you automatically know a solution or a new direction, do not tell the employer right then and there, because you will be making an unfavorable impression as a know-it-all. Instead, say that you would like to think about it and call the interviewer back in a day or two. If you are able to come up with an effective solution for a potential employer and can prove how you were held in high regard by former employers, you will be well on your way to landing a job.

That is exactly what happened to a manager in the computer programming industry. During an interview, an employer described a problem that had occurred in the design of a new program. He asked the job candidate if he could think of a solution. The interviewee said he wanted to give it more thought and asked if he could take it home and call the employer back in a day or two. The interviewer agreed. Two days later, the job candidate called the employer and said he had come up with a solution to the problem and would like to meet to discuss it. An appointment was arranged for the next day. The interviewer told the job candidate that he was very pleased with his careful consideration and asked him to come for another interview later that week.

Solving problems this way absolutely sets you apart from the competition. How many other applicants do you suppose saw the same opportunity and did the same thinking? Few, I believe, would be so willing to show their interest in the company and its problems.

Discuss Salary and Benefits Only When Asked

Although salary and benefits are a taboo topic (if they can be avoided) in interview number one, the discussion will inevitably turn to money and benefits once the person with hiring authority decides to offer you the job. Avoid the subject of salary until an offer is on the table. If you raise the subject of salary first, you are implying that your main concern is yourself, not the company or the job. In most cases, that will remove you from consideration for the job.

As you increase your visibility with the prospective employer, he or she likes you more and the price goes up. You reach the point where the subject of money will require only a gentle nudge on your part after a job offer is made, and you should be able to get what you require. For specific pointers on negotiating a salary, see Chapter 15.

Offer to Work Free for 30 Days

If dozens of interviews have not led to an offer and you can afford it, you may want to offer to work free for a company for 30 days. This offer should only be made on a selective basis to a company for which you definitely want to work. You need to be confident that you can get the job done and prove yourself to the prospective employer within that time period. If the prospective employer accepts the offer, three important objectives must be accomplished during those 30 days.

1. Whatever you promised to do for the employer, you must do. The prospective employer will be monitoring your actions closely; if it is apparent that you are not fulfilling what you promised, you will not get the offer.

2. Look for problem-solving opportunities. Keep your eyes and ears open for potential or existing problems and then take responsibility for personally finding solutions for them.

3. Make it a point to build a good rapport with your coworkers. You need to be a team player and be well liked by others in order to succeed.

Chapter 14

After the Interview: Assessment and Follow-Up

ALTHOUGH THE INTERVIEW is the most important part of the job search, your work does not end when an interview is concluded. Many job seekers make the mistake of thinking that when a job interview is over, the only thing they need do is sit back and wait for a yes or no response from the potential employer. Instead, you should follow the same advice in the postinterview stage as in the preinterview stage: never sit back and wait for something to happen. It probably won't!

Employers seldom make a job offer in the first interview. They interview several candidates for a given position and often hold two or more rounds of interviews before making an offer. Therefore, what you do after the first interview can have a direct bearing on whether you will be asked back for successive interviews.

By staying in contact with the employer through telephone calls and letters, you can continue to sell yourself by proving your interest in a job and demonstrating your value and worth to the company. First, however, you need to review your performance in each interview.

Review and Assess Your Interview

After you finish an interview, find a quiet place where you can go over the interview in your mind. Take the time to identify its high and low points. Reflect on the company's needs and how well you were able to demonstrate that you meet them. Try to think of examples you may have left out that show how you contributed to the advancement of a previous employer's business. Write down your thoughts so you do not confuse interviews and companies two or three weeks later. Also, your reflection will help you write a better follow-up letter and prepare you for subsequent interviews, whether with the same company or a different one.

Trust your hunch about an interview. If you feel it went well, it probably did. If you liked the interviewer, the interviewer probably liked you, because the feelings are almost invariably mutual. If you did not enjoy the interview or like the person, something probably went wrong.

Taking the time to go over an interview paid off for one discharged manager. He realized that he had left out an example regarding a new marketing plan he had developed at a previous job. From the direction the interview had taken, he thought the example would be just the kind of information that would interest the employer. Instead of taking a passive approach by sitting back and hoping he would be invited back for a second interview, he took an active approach and included the example in his thank-you letter. After the employer read the letter, he was asked back for a second interview. During the interview, the employer made specific reference to the example the applicant had cited in his letter as showing the type of skills for which the company was looking. A week later, he was hired.

Reviewing Your Performance

As you reflect on an interview, answer these questions:

- Did you and the interviewer get along?
- If not, why?

- What did you do or say that may have closed a door?
- What actions, statements, or mannerisms turned off the interviewer?
- What are the company's needs as you perceive them?
- Which accomplishments did you relate to those needs?
- Was there anything you neglected to mention?
- Did you demonstrate your expertise?
- Did you talk too much?
- Did you ask for the order?

The Postinterview Follow-Up

Job seekers often complain about employers who do not acknowledge their calls, letters, even their interviews. "I sent out hundreds of resumes and have yet to hear back from anyone," they say. "They at least owe me a letter or a phone call." That notion could not be further from reality. The interviewer's only mission is to find the right person as soon as possible. Job seekers like you are unfortunately owed nothing. Interviewers have no moral or business courtesy obligation to acknowledge anything. That is realism.

Consider the follow-up an integral step in the job search process, whether it is after sending a resume, talking on the phone, or having a formal interview. It can provide a very competitive edge. Few people believe they should or "are allowed" to follow up. One company told me it received 40 resumes for a job, and only one person bothered to call to see about an interview!

If you are lining up interviews, you will need to call the company in order to find out whether you have a chance for an interview. If you have already been through an interview, you need to sit down and write a gracious thank-you letter to the person with whom you interviewed. Do not send the letter immediately after the interview; wait several days so the interviewer will remember you in the following weeks.

In all follow-up correspondence or conversations, you need to stress two points. First, tell the interviewer that the job sounded wonderful and that you want to work for the company. Second, repeat your main qualifications. You want to keep yourself and your accomplishments foremost in the interviewer's mind until a decision to hire is made, while reminding the person that you are enthusiastic and eager to join the company team.

Follow Up by Telephone

After sending the letter, keep in touch with the interviewer by telephone on a regular basis. Call him or her every week to 10 days. Be persistent, but not annoying. Use good judgment. It is better, however, to err on the side of being too aggressive rather than too respectful if, in the name of respect, you become too passive. The more you can talk to the interviewer, the greater your chances of being hired.

Project a positive attitude on the phone and let the potential employer know you are still very interested in the position. If he or she says a decision has yet to be made but does not mention anything about following up, say you will check back.

When you call an employer to follow up, ask if there is any additional information you can provide. Asking this question may create new opportunities. For example, one electrical engineering executive placed a follow-up call a week after a potential employer received his thank-you letter. The employer said a few other candidates for the position were still being interviewed, and that a decision would not be made for at least another week. Instead of being discouraged and hanging up, the job seeker asked if there was any additional information he could provide. It opened a new dialogue. Since the original interview, the company had decided to develop a new product. After describing it briefly, the interviewer asked the job seeker if he had any ideas for its design. The job seeker responded enthusiastically and asked if he could think about it and see her in a couple of days with some suggestions. As promised, two days later the job seeker came back and discussed his ideas. When he was done, the employer was very impressed and offered him the position.

Your follow-up call need not focus exclusively on additional information. You can also use it to stress information you have already presented. If your accomplishments and qualifications are particularly well suited to the job, take advantage of the opportunity and say so all over again. Stating the same message in a new way helps the interviewer remember you.

Try never to leave a message when you follow up. If you cannot reach the interviewer, keep attempting until you get him or her on the phone. However, sometimes you need to read the writing on the wall. It takes an average of four telephone calls to reach most executives and managers. If you have called eight or nine times without reaching the person you need to talk to, he or she may be trying to push you away. On the other hand, the person may simply still be interviewing. Try once or twice more before abandoning your quest.

There is no need to be fearful or intimidated about the follow-up process. The most common excuse individuals cite about not following up is that they fear rejection. Job seekers believe it is easier to accept rejection if they hear nothing at all than it is to get the final "Thanks, but no thanks" over the phone. Make them reject you even though it might make you feel bad.

Although "no" can be hard to hear, it brings to a close a job possibility which you were hoping would come to fruition and which may have held you back from going full force in your job search. Also, just because you were not right for one position does not mean you may not be a candidate for another position at the same company. Ask the person with whom you interviewed or to whom you sent your resume if there are other positions where someone with your energy, commitment, and skills would fit. See if there are other hiring managers you could meet.

By following up before you secure an interview, you might find out that the person never got your resume or call in the first place. Fax machines, the mail service, voice mail, and secretaries are by no means foolproof. Following up also sends a signal that you are interested and eager to get a position. Remember the story about how only one person out of 40 followed up after sending a resume? That person secured an interview!

Ask for Referrals

If, during a follow-up call, an employer tells you there is no opportunity for you with that company, thank the individual for his or her time and ask for referrals to other companies. Using the referral tactic benefited one marketing executive. He had interviewed with five companies and learned in follow-up calls that there was no opportunity for him at two of them. The other three had yet to decide. Instead of seeing dead ends, he saw opportunities. He thanked the two employers for their time and asked if they could give him contacts at other companies. Having the presence of mind to ask this one question created several new avenues for him to pursue. He was given five new leads, three of which were at companies that were hiring.

Even if a particular company says it is not hiring, job openings are often created on the spot. If that does not happen, you still may be able to get additional leads. When you call each new contact, use the name of the employer who referred you. Using such referrals enabled one marketing executive to set up interviews with several new leads. During the course of an interview with one company that said it was not hiring, an opportunity arose. The employer described a problem the company was having in the repositioning of an old product. The job seeker did not offer an immediate solution to the problem, but discussed his experience with similar projects for previous employers. Liking what he heard, the employer later asked the job seeker to come back for a second interview. During that interview, the job seeker was offered a job—one that had been created because his expertise directly fit the needs of the company.

Determined job seekers get the job because they go by the motto, "It's not over till it's over."

Keep an Open Mind

There are some job leads you will not be able to anticipate. Therefore you should always end a conversation or an interview with a prospective employer on a positive, upbeat note, regardless of whether you are offered or are being considered for a job. Never turn down a chance to meet with someone because you never know where your next job lead will come from.

For example, an executive from the computer industry followed up with a prospective employer after an interview and learned that someone else had been hired. The prospective employer said he was sorry it did not work out, but that he would keep him in mind. The job seeker thought he was just trying to be kind and figured he had reached a dead end with him. Although he was let down, he thanked the prospective employer for the interview and wrote a note of appreciation for the employer's consideration. A week later, he received a call on his answering machine from another employer in the computer industry. Much to his surprise, the prospective employer said his name had been referred by the employer with whom he had interviewed the week before. The employer had meant what he said about keeping the applicant in mind. He arranged for an interview later in the week.

Schedule Interviews Until You Are Hired

While you are following up on interviews, do not back off on scheduling new ones. Like the Energizer Bunny, you need to keep going and going and going until you get the job offer. You cannot let your job search hinge on one company or one job. Nothing is a done deal until it is completed. Do not take anything for granted, and do not wait for an anticipated job offer. Keep interviewing as if the possibility did not exist. You need to create as many opportunities as you can. The worst thing that could happen is that you receive more than one job offer.

How carefully you follow up after an interview can distinguish you from competitors who follow up less or not at all. When you call, it says that you are interested, that follow-up is part of your personal style, that you are aggressive and go after what you want. That action is a strong, positive message to send about yourself. Make follow-up a cornerstone of your job search.

Chapter 15

Evaluating Offers and Negotiating Salary

IF YOU ARE diligent about going out on interviews, you will eventually be offered a job. An offer gives you a bargaining edge with the employer. That individual has demonstrated that he or she likes you and wants you to work for the company. You now have leverage in negotiating salary, benefits, and whatever other workplace factors may be important to you.

Before you decide to move forward, however, you need to decide whether the job is for you.

Evaluating an Offer

Job offers tend to come in ones. Few people have a choice between two or more job offers at the same time. Although it is natural to want to accept the first position offered, do not let the prospect and excitement of getting a job cloud the real issues of how happy you would be in that job. You may be flattered and your ego inflated by someone being interested in hiring you, but if you feel that it is not a good fit, it may be best to walk away. You will create other opportunities for job offers with companies for which you are better suited.

Remember, a job is like a marriage. Your personality and the company's personality have to mesh. It is important to determine the quality of the match before accepting a job. In their haste to become reemployed as quickly as possible, many job seekers ignore obvious differences or hope that those differences can be ironed out later. As in a marriage of spouses with unresolved conflicts, this melding does not usually happen.

If you have done the self-appraisal exercises outlined in Chapter 6, you should have a good handle on the kind of job you are looking for. Do not rush into something that will not work for you. If you do, conflicts will soon arise. Differences between you and your employer are likely to manifest themselves in a negative way. Your performance may not be up to par because you are not satisfied with the work arrangement. If the differences are not settled, you may be discharged and you will have to start over from scratch.

One discharged advertising agency executive had worked in an atmosphere that fostered creativity. He had also worked predominantly on group assignments and was accustomed to an atmosphere that was casual in attitude and dress. During one interview, when the employer talked about the structure of the firm, the account executive realized he would often work alone and that most of his work would be predefined. Subsequently receiving an offer, he went home and weighed everything in his mind. He tried to imagine what it would be like if he accepted the position. He realized that his job performance would be hampered and that he would be unhappy with the new role, so he decided, despite the fact that the job would pay him an equivalent salary, to reject the offer. In a later interview, the account executive met with an organization offering the kind of work atmosphere he was after. His enthusiasm and experience came through and he was offered a job.

The key is to be completely honest with yourself. Courageously recognizing that he would not be successful in the first job he was offered saved this man later heartache and also enabled him to focus his job search more sharply than ever.

Another way to determine whether or not a company is a good match is to keep your eyes and ears open as you walk through the office to your interview. If compatibility is important to you, ask yourself the following questions:

- Do you get a good feeling as you walk around?
- Do the people seem friendly?
- Do you feel comfortable?
- Are people working together and discussing business openly, or are they working in solitude?
- Can you picture yourself working there?

The best way to ensure that the job you are offered is the right job at the right company is to compare it to the self-assessment you completed at the outset of your job search. It is easy to be so excited by a job offer that you forget to look candidly at your likes, dislikes, strengths, and values, all of which determine the conditions under which you work best. That is one reason you assess before you look. It allows you to effectively appraise a potential employer. If a job you are thinking of accepting has objectionable aspects that may keep you from performing at your highest level, your self-assessment may give you the courage to turn it down.

Negotiating Tips

- Establish your minimum salary requirement before you begin to interview, but keep it to yourself.

- Let the interviewer be the first to raise the subject and state a salary figure.

- Never ask for less than your previous earnings.

- Do not let an attractive salary persuade you to accept a job you will dislike.

How to Negotiate Like a Pro

Obviously, questions regarding salary and benefits may be important when you apply for a job. If possible, however, they should not be discussed until your second, third, or fourth interview. Remember, your salary requirements are not the employer's main concern. The hiring executive is more interested in what you can do for the company and why you should be hired over several other candidates who appear to be equally qualified. Therefore, your goal in the first interview should be to make a good impression on the interviewer. If you do that, it is likely that you will be asked back for subsequent interviews. If you do not, forget about the job.

Be patient. The discussion will inevitably turn to money and benefits in successive interviews, if the person with hiring authority decides to offer you the job. Unfortunately, many applicants overlook the basic fact, emphasized throughout this book, that the objective of the job search is to get the offer. All efforts should be directed toward that central goal, beginning with your first contact with the prospective employer. You may decide after the offer is made not to accept the job. If you leave the wrong impression after the first meeting, you may never have that choice to make. After the offer is made, not before, is the time to start discussing salary.

Consider the case of Allan, who interviewed for the position of account executive at a large advertising agency. He was particularly concerned about money because of his high overhead. In his previous position, he had accumulated considerable debt under the belief that he was in line for a significant raise in the near future. His family had moved to a larger home and his children had entered college.

Unfortunately, Allan's previous employer had suddenly suffered major and unexpected business losses, and Allan had been discharged. During Allan's first job interview, the hiring executive was familiar with Allan's work and was pleased with his background. However, Allan sabotaged the good rapport he began to build by raising the topic of money too early. He stated that he admired the agency's work, but could not accept less than a certain salary level. As it turned out, he had to accept a lot less. He was eliminated as a candidate because, in effect, he told the employer that his primary concern was money, not the job opportunity or the agency.

In some cases, the hiring executive may raise the subject of money in the first interview with a question such as, "What will it take to get you here?" or "How much of a salary are you looking for?" You cannot ignore the question if it is specifically raised. Nevertheless, try not to ask for a specific salary; merely state your current or last salary, which does not commit you to a particular figure. Or you may give an innocuous response such as, "I am looking for a salary comparable to my experience or skills." Then switch the subject back to the job at hand. Both answers give the impression that money is not the main reason for your job search.

If you name a salary figure that is much too high, you will price yourself out of the job and indicate that you will be dissatisfied with less. On the other hand, if you give too low a figure, the employer will tend to think the job is too big for you and may question your competence. In addition, if the employer is first to name a figure, the negotiation can be directed toward increasing salary or adding concessions. However, if you are the first to name a figure, in most cases the negotiation will probably be about decreasing it.

If the hiring executive offers a salary figure that is too low, do not hesitate to let him or her know, but *not* at that interview. Take the offer home and then come back again and haggle. Start by pointing out that you want to work for the company. Then explain why you cannot accept an amount below your minimum salary requirement. If the employer has relaxed by thinking you are coming to the company, he or she will not want to be wrong. Waiting for a later interview puts you in a stronger bargaining posture.

The employer knows others will be applying for the same position and may be fishing for the lowest salary you will accept. Stick to your predetermined minimum salary requirement. The job market is strong and receptive for qualified individuals, and there are other jobs that will meet your needs if this one does not.

Never Ask for Less

A common mistake made by people looking for work is to lower their salary request. Virtually all job applicants who lower their salary prospects below previous earning levels think they are making themselves more appealing by asking for less, particularly now, and they expect to be viewed more positively by employers if they do.

However, the effect is just the opposite. All you are doing is damaging your chances of being hired and prolonging the job search. Unfortunately, if you ask for less, you are viewed by employers as being "undesirable property" or as someone who was previously overpaid. Obviously, if employers view you as undesirable or anything other than a first-class prospect, you are not likely to be hired.

What you earned on your last job is what you are worth. It is your true market value. When you lower your salary request to an employer, you are sending a message that you really do not have much confidence in yourself. The employer may interpret that to mean that you may be indecisive, tentative, slow to take action, and the type to avoid showing initiative. Alternatively, many employers connote salary with capability. If you ask for less, you are indicating self-doubts about your ability.

This is definitely not the sort of message you want to send to a prospective employer. You want to position yourself as being confident, self-assured, able to step forward and take command of the situation. Asking for less money than you made on your previous job also may give the prospective employer the impression that you have low self-esteem. When you do not have a high opinion of yourself, how can you possibly convince an employer to have a high opinion of you?

Most employers really do not want to hire people at bargain basement prices, and you should seriously question your future with a company that attempts to buy you for less than your true worth. The money a company saves in this way will cost them much more in the long run if the employee does not work out or makes serious mistakes that disrupt work harmony or irritate customers. A company that tries to get you for less may continue to treat you in a bargain basement fashion after you are hired, perhaps by underfunding your operation.

The majority of employers will avoid the "penny wise and pound foolish" philosophy. They know their best interests lie in obtaining the best qualified individual they can for the job. An important requirement in realizing that objective is to establish a realistic salary scale. Also, employers who know they have hired a manager too cheaply worry that a better offer by another firm can easily lure that manager away.

As I have stressed numerous times, the bottom line in job search success is being liked in the interview. When you are liked in the first interview, you will be asked to return for successive interviews. As you increase your visibility with the prospective employer, he or she likes you more and the price goes up. You reach the point where the subject of money will require only a gentle nudge on your part after a job offer is made, and you should be able to get what you require.

One note of caution: if, after you find out more about the job, you decide you do not like it, do not be tempted to take it just because the employer is offering you a good salary. Your discontent will quickly become evident once you are on the job, regardless of how much money you are getting. You may try to rationalize to yourself, "Well, I could learn to like it," but that is not likely. Do yourself and the employer a favor by continuing your job search elsewhere.

Employers have salary schedules and budgets and know what they can pay for each position. They are more than willing to meet the salary demands of those they want to hire. A few thousand dollars will make little difference to the corporation in the long run.

Part IV

MANAGING YOUR CAREER

MANY CHALLENGER clients are surprised to hear that landing a new job is no reason to stop marketing themselves. Job advancement is no longer automatic; ascending the career ladder requires just as much thought and strategy as landing a job. In this section, you will learn how to manage your career by developing and marketing your strengths and skills to your employer. You will also discover the basic requirements for success in entrepreneurship, an increasingly popular alternative to conventional full-time employment.

Chapter 16

Take Charge of Your Career—No One Else Will

CONGRATULATIONS. You got the job. Now what?

Just a few years ago, it was easy to see where you were going in a company and how you were going to get there. Most companies had a vertical organization and your career path was clearly laid out for you. The company had a paternalistic approach to an employee's career. Your employer would tell you what you needed to do to get to the next level and, if you were liked and dedicated, generally helped you get there. A promotion and a salary increase came your way every few years to acknowledge your adequate or good work.

Those days have vanished. Technology, reengineering, downsizing, and global competition have changed the way individuals move up through the company ranks. The responsibility for your future within a company no longer rests with the employer. What you make of your career in a company rests squarely on your shoulders.

Reengineering, by nature, is designed to bring about a less structured workplace. Once these changes take root, the inevitable result is that individuals not only have more autonomy over the functions they perform, but also are more responsible than ever for their own career paths. Moreover, global competition and a never-ending quest by companies to slash costs have fundamentally changed the workplace. While dedication and competence are expected, they no longer ensure that an employee will keep his or her job, much less secure a promotion.

A new set of motivational factors is driving today's workplace. Because competition forces employers to move faster than ever, most companies can no longer lay clear ground rules for what they expect from employees over the long term. The stark reality is that most companies no longer promise or guarantee long-time employment to even the most dedicated, hard-working individuals and in return do not really demand ultimate loyalty.

The rules have changed. It is your job to develop your strengths and skills and constantly market yourself to your employer. If you are aware of this right from the start and take control of your work life, you will advance more quickly and be paid more money than those who wait for the company to tell them what to do.

Four strategies will help you manage your career successfully:

- See yourself as a provider of services.
- Make yourself more valuable.
- Seek recognition for your accomplishments.
- Adapt to corporate change.

See Yourself as a Provider of Services

As I explained in Chapter 5, you are not an employee. You are a provider of services whose experience is a valuable commodity. An employee of the company can be hired—and discharged—at any time by the employer. A provider of services is someone in charge of his or her own destiny who possesses particular skills that can help many companies.

An employee sits back and says, "Okay, you hired me, now what do you want me to do?" A provider of services has replaced this old-fashioned, defensive attitude with a more proactive approach. You know you were hired because your particular knowledge and work experience benefits the company. To stay on the payroll, you need to concentrate on developing and utilizing your skills and knowledge to prove to your employer that your services are invaluable.

As a provider of services, you need to look at your company and its employees in a different light.

Understand How Your Expertise Contributes to Your Company's Bottom Line

To be a provider of services, you need to find out how your expertise contributes to the company's bottom line. Many individuals go to work each day without ever asking, "How do I make maximum impact upon the company's financial performance?" They are apt to be the same people who do not understand why they are not moving up the organization or are being laid off.

By learning how your department, position, and individual skills help the company's bottom line, you are better able to assess your value to the company. You can then plan what new skills or knowledge you will need to acquire to enhance your value to the company, and map out a strategy for ways to increase your impact or seek out other companies where your skills will be more appreciated.

To move up in your company, start thinking like a top-level executive and focus on the bottom line.

Create Good Relationships

Although thinking of yourself as a provider of services means concentrating on the skills you provide, it does not lessen the importance of forging a good relationship with your boss. More people are discharged from a job because they did not get along with their employer than because of a performance issue. It is up to *you* to get along with your boss. It is not his or her job.

First and foremost, you have to be liked. You were liked when you were hired, but rapport with your employer will not continue automatically. You must consciously work at it. It is easy to fall out of favor if you become careless or overconfident. That is when you are most likely to make mistakes that will downgrade you in the eyes of your supervisor. Do not let it happen. Review what it is the employer liked about you when you were hired and keep up those qualities.

You need to talk openly and often with your boss about all aspects of the job. Let your boss know what you are doing at all times and inquire as to what skills you may need to improve or new ones you should obtain.

Relationships with your coworkers also are important. Remember, your office is a community as well as a place of business. The relationships you develop are crucial both now and in future organizations.

How to Make Yourself More Valuable

- Learn other functions within your organization.
- Identify and solve problems in your department or elsewhere in the organization.
- Volunteer for additional work, including civic and charitable activities.
- Stay late and come in early.
- Continually assess your performance and seek ways to improve.
- Acquire new skills and update old ones.
- Master new technologies and business practices.

Make Yourself More Valuable

The best way to advance in a company? Do everything you can to make yourself a more valuable provider of services!

Learn Other Functions Within the Organization

The sooner you can learn about operational practices within the company, the faster you will progress and the more secure your future will be. Most senior-level managers did not get where they are by specializing in one area. Without stepping on others' toes and letting your current responsibilities suffer, make it a personal challenge to learn as much as you can as quickly as possible.

People who can do more than one job are valued everywhere, especially in small to medium-sized companies that need people who can wear more than one hat to help them compete effectively. If you were hired for one particular skill and possess others that have not yet been used at your company, mention them to your supervisor. Your willingness to undertake additional responsibilities will mark you as an individual who is concerned with the company's needs and welfare.

Tackle Problems

Look around you for problem areas that need attention in your department or elsewhere in the company. Obviously you do not want to tell someone else how to do his or her job, but virtually all companies welcome employee suggestions. If you can come up with a solution to a profit-draining problem or provide some assistance in an emergency situation, you may quickly win the approval of senior management. Look for new marketing directions or seek ways to reduce operating expenses or improve efficiencies. Businesses everywhere are emphasizing cost-effective ways of doing things.

While a potential hire should *never* presume to tell the company how to do a better job, a long-time employee has an obligation to do so. Capitalize on your familiarity with the company and its operations, roll up your sleeves, and get to work solving problems.

Volunteer for Additional Work

Without making it appear that you are bucking for a promotion, volunteer for additional assignments. There are numerous opportunities to increase your visibility in the company and gain increased appreciation of yourself as a valued employee. Consider extra job-related responsibilities as well as the company's community relations activities and fund drives for charitable organizations.

One strategy is to find out your supervisor's favorite civic or charitable activities and volunteer to work for those organizations. These activities will bring you into regular contact with your supervisor in a nonjob situation, which should increase your visibility and give you additional opportunities to make a favorable impression. Developing some shared activities off the job will be a definite plus for you.

It sounds pretty basic, but this is one principle that will never change. There is no better way to remain visible within the organization than by making yourself available whenever and wherever you are needed. It is one thing to agree to put in the extra effort when asked, but management will take notice when you volunteer your time, effort, and ideas.

Stay Late and Come In Early

Make it a point to observe when your supervisor arrives in the morning and how late he or she works. Adapt your own hours to the same schedule. If your supervisor puts in weekend hours, ask if there is anything you can do to help. It may provide you with an opportunity to increase your rapport in a more relaxed atmosphere than during the regular workweek. In any case, your boss will appreciate the fact that you are willing to put the interests of the company first by putting in extra time.

Conduct Continuous Self-Assessment

Stay a step ahead of the performance appraisal and review process by continually monitoring your own performance. Keep your own personal performance chart and review it regularly to see how you can improve your contributions to the company.

Once a week (over the weekend when you have some leisure is the best time), sit down with your chart and make notes for yourself. Ask yourself these kinds of questions:

- What did you accomplish in the past week that you were especially proud of?
- In what ways could you have improved what you did?

- Did you have some areas of conflict during the week?
- How could you have resolved those situations better?

Ask yourself these questions regularly. If you do not keep up the process of self-examination, you are likely to become complacent about your performance. Employers want people who are looking for better ways to do their jobs and increase their productivity, not those who just coast along.

Take stock of where you are in the company. What do you do for your employer and how does it help attain his or her goals? The closer you are to helping your company reach its objectives, the higher your value to the company. What else can you do?

When you receive your formal evaluation, carefully note your strengths and weaknesses as the company sees them. Your first reaction may be to dispute what the company is saying about you, but that is an unwise course of action. If the review is not as favorable as you would like, think of ways to make the next one more favorable. The review you have just had is not going to be changed. The company, rightly or wrongly, has formed certain conclusions about you. It is up to you to profit from what you have learned. Rather than becoming defensive about any criticisms, take that opportunity to ask your supervisor how you can improve your performance.

Improve Your Skills

Take night courses to learn new ways of doing things; educate yourself on the newest techniques and skills. Take advantage of any training offered by your company and ask whether you can be reimbursed for outside courses. If you can bring new ideas or improved ways of doing things to your company, your value will increase significantly.

Stay Current with New Technology

It is imperative to stay current with new technology and state-of-the-art business practices in your field. Your education was just beginning when you graduated from school! If you have been in the workforce for a number of years, do not get lulled into a false sense of complacency or believe that the "experience factor" will win out every time when competing for a new job or holding on to the one you have. If a younger individual can show that he or she can provide the same services as you, despite the difference in working years, you may lose out because of "price competition."

The Rewards of Becoming More Valuable

An account manager, selected by her boss to represent him at a conference, was chosen over 15 others, some of whom held higher positions. How she landed the plum assignment of standing in for the boss is a case study in the new approach to managing your own career.

The account manager—let's call her Nancy—had consistently shown her employer and manager that she was willing to go that extra mile for the good of the company, even without being asked. She proved this time and again by volunteering for assignments. In one instance, she and the other account managers in her department heard that the company had just acquired a new account that one of the managers would be asked to take on and direct. While the other managers were griping about the prospect of more work, Nancy went to her manager and volunteered for the extra assignment. After staying late and reading over the proposal for the new project, she recognized problems in its structure. Without being asked, she wrote an outline that offered solutions and presented it to her manager the next morning before she even started the new project. No wonder she earned the increased respect of her superiors and was singled out to represent the boss at the conference.

Find Job Openings Within the Company

Many companies use internal job posting to keep job searches limited to current employees. As they open up, stay on top of new positions that would put you in a more advantageous situation within the company. If you cannot move up within your own department, look elsewhere in the company for opportunities.

Seek Recognition for Your Accomplishments

It is only natural to want recognition. It is an important part of your "psychic income," the elements of the job not concerned with benefits or money. Also, recognition is a prerequisite for advancing in a company. It is not enough to do a good job and hope that someone notices or appreciates it.

When recognition is withheld or is erroneously granted to someone else, you may feel slighted and unfairly treated. As a result, resentments can build up, eventually hampering your performance and serving as a roadblock to advancement in the company. If you do not feel you are getting the recognition you deserve, do not complain about it to your coworkers. It only creates tension in the workplace and brands you with the undesirable reputation of being a complainer that may follow you from job to job.

It is your job to tell others about your work so your accomplishments can be acknowledged. Use the following steps to ensure that you get the full recognition your work deserves.

Document How Your Job Contributes to the Bottom Line

All work accomplishes one of three goals:

- It increases the company's visibility in the marketplace.
- It increases the company's market share.
- It increases the company's profitability.

In some cases, more than one category applies. Think about how your job meets these criteria. What do you do that increases visibility, market share, or profitability? Keep a list of your assignments or projects and tie each one you accomplish to one of these three goals.

Communicate Your Accomplishments

Plan regular meetings with your boss and state what you have done. Be sure to mention well-thought-out new ideas and suggestions for improving the bottom line. The company does not necessarily know what you have done for it lately, and in many cases good work can go unrecognized if you do not call it to your superiors' attention.

Although some people prefer to send memos or notes about what they are doing, written materials may not be read by the intended source. It is far better to discuss your accomplishments in person. Bring along a written report if you want, but use it as a backup to your conversation or leave it with your supervisor when you go.

If you work in a branch location and your direct manager is at the corporate headquarters, the situation is a bit more difficult. However, instead of sending memos, seek reasons to see the individual in person.

Do not be shy! Letting people know what you are doing and what you have accomplished is not a bad thing, whether you are interviewing for a new job or working your way up the corporate hierarchy. Your work life is a constant sales job. You must sell yourself like a product to win a job. Once you have joined a company, you need to continually promote yourself and your accomplishments to hold on to your job and move through the corporate ranks.

Never assume that your accomplishments are known by individuals higher up in the company. While you may think your successes and achievements are highly visible, remember that you are only one of many people in the company. Many times the layers of management who might have known about your contributions either leave the company or are busy fighting their own battles. Take every opportunity you can to sell yourself and your accomplishments to those above you.

Telecommuting? Don't Become an Invisible Worker

Phyllis was offered an opportunity that appeared ideal: the chance to avoid a lengthy and traffic-choked daily commute by working from home via computer. She worked for several months from home, sending and receiving instructions electronically and occasionally calling the office on the phone. She enjoyed her newfound flexibility.

Then one day she went to the office for a meeting and found to her surprise that she had missed a planning session that previously she had regularly attended. When she asked why she had not been notified about it, the manager who set it up remarked, "Well, since we don't see much of you anymore, we didn't think of asking you."

The lesson to be learned here is that, while telecommuting may seem to offer exceptional lifestyle conveniences, it can be a minefield if it leads to loss of workplace visibility. Employers usually do not take into their confidence people they rarely see. They are not even thought about in the same manner as coworkers who are visible every day. The telecommuter can become as dispensable as an on-call consultant who is not considered a colleague but a resource.

The loss of visibility impacts greatly on personal advancement. One of the cardinal rules for advancement is to seek out critical assignments that offer high exposure within the organization. For example, it is better to work at a corporate headquarters than at a remote location or branch. The person who is at the center of decision making has a much better opportunity to be an "insider."

The telecommuter is like a manager assigned to an international post. They both have the same problem: they cannot greet their employer personally in the morning or hold a casual conversation over coffee during the celebration of a coworker's birthday. No personal relationship develops; it is all electronic. Without the opportunity for interaction with coworkers, the individual is limited. Employees who are in day-to-day personal contact are much more likely to be targeted for promotions.

If you telecommute, you need to find every possible way to appear to be in two places at once so you are not referred to as someone who "works away from the office." Over time, that phrase confers a negative status that can wear away any previous workplace relationship you may have established. You need to find ways to perform the work well and plan and present your work in a way that maintains your workplace visibility and fosters the impression of maintaining a daily presence at the office.

- Know meeting schedules in advance. Arrange a telecommuting schedule by working around office meetings. Get early access to the meeting schedule so you do not miss a single one.
- Find reasons to visit the office often. Avoid sending reports electronically if the report has never been handled without a face-to-face meeting. Either get it done early to coincide with the due date or arrange a meeting in advance of its due date to present it in person.
- Attend special office events. Show up for social and athletic events, anniversaries, and other key events.
- Arrange to have office memos e-mailed to you or mailed to your home address, even on days you are in the office.
- Install an answering machine or buy a pager so you do not miss any business calls.
- Call the office several times a day on days when you are working from home.
- Keep your boss informed, in person, about your accomplishments. Although the electronic evidence may summarize what you have done, there is no substitute for a personal discussion with your manager to cite your accomplishments.

Adapt to Corporate Change

Company priorities change rapidly. By anticipating changes and planning for them, you can benefit from them instead of being caught off guard when they occur.

The clues of organizational change are obvious once you look for them. Products or services may be dropped; job functions, management, or entire departments may be realigned. If a profitable division is being sold, it could mean the rest of the company is in financial difficulty and the sale of the division is being used to prop up operating income. If a product is selling well but losing market share to the competition, trouble may lie ahead.

If you see any of these clues, be assertive and ask about their impact on your department or position. You cannot be faulted for taking an active interest in your job and the company's welfare. Do not wait for the change to occur and then try to adapt, or the parade may pass you by. Plan for change instead.

One midlevel marketing manager saw that some of his company's product lines were not doing well in relation to their competitors and figured it was only a matter of time until they were modified or discontinued altogether. The question was, what types of products would replace them? In conversations with senior executives, his hunches were confirmed. Although nothing was said directly about the coming changes, he gained enough insight to make an educated guess. He began jotting down ideas in his spare time about how he would market the new products. He also did research on how similar products had been marketed by other firms, noting their successes and failures. He was under no pressure to do this within any particular time frame because the company had made no moves. He correctly assumed that when the move came, it would come very quickly.

The announcement of a major change in the direction of several product lines was made overnight, catching many people at the company by surprise. The marketing manager was prepared, however. He already had a plan for marketing the new products and was able to go immediately to a top executive and discuss his ideas. He made an excellent impression on his superiors all the way up to the senior executive suite. He was lauded for his perception and initiative, putting him in line for both a raise and a promotion.

More and more, this type of initiative is what will be required in order to stand out in companies that are under increasing pressure to improve profits. There is certainly more stress in the workplace, but along with that stress come opportunities to stand out. As products, methods, and personnel change, so do managerial goals and expectations. Successful workers not only anticipate how these changes will affect their duties but also try to incorporate them into their functions as smoothly and efficiently as possible. Your ability to adapt and successfully meet new requirements is a valuable commodity.

When Is It Time to Move On?

Under what circumstances should you seek a position at another company? If you learn that your company is a candidate for acquiring another firm or is being bought out itself, it is time to seriously and honestly assess your current position, or someone else may do it for you. When a company is merged or acquired, the new management will immediately make changes in the employee ranks. Individuals who fill positions the new company needs will be retained. Those who duplicate responsibilities already being handled by the acquiring company are likely to be discharged.

If you know that your company's business has been down for a period of time and if your company is closing manufacturing plants, shutting distribution centers, and in general contracting its business, management is probably looking for places to cut. Your job could be next.

Also, pay attention to those individuals who joined the firm in the same position and at the same time you did. Are they getting promotions faster than you? Are their responsibilities different or more significant than yours? If the answer is yes, then you should realistically look at what the future holds for you at that company.

Similarly, your job may not be in jeopardy, but you may feel that you are stagnating. Often companies that are looking hard at their bottom line may not be promoting as fast or giving significant salary increases. The only way to improve your position and the money you make may be by seeking out positions at other companies.

However, be careful about being too quick to leave your current job. In these days of ongoing mergers and downsizings, the company you are considering going to work for may be a merger candidate itself. Before you take another job, investigate as best you can the new firm's financial situation and whether there are rumors of a buyout.

The bottom line in changing jobs—either by moving up your company's hierarchy or changing companies altogether—is to take control of your destiny. Competition is doing its job. It is forcing business to become more efficient, lower costs, and produce better products. In the process, business is eliminating antiquated ways of operating, including the blueprint for career advancement. Responsibilities and divisions of duty have become blurred. Risk-takers are at a premium. To succeed in this climate, you need to take responsibility for your own career path and ultimately your success or failure.

Chapter 17

Should You Start Your Own Business?

NOT EVERYONE WHO has been downsized or discharged wants to continue in today's competitive job marketplace. More and more of the people my counselors see are interested in starting their own business instead.

Starting your own business is an excellent alternative if you have the right qualifications and necessary amount of energy. The economic climate for entrepreneurship is very bullish right now. New company start-ups are increasing. Fewer new businesses are failing, while total incorporations are strong, increasing the number of net formations.

Why Entrepreneurship Is on the Rise

There are several reasons behind the surge in entrepreneurship.

Downsizing

A major force behind the acceleration in entrepreneurship is downsizing. Many people, upset about losing a job, do not want to place themselves in a similar position again. They want to be in charge of their own destiny—a most understandable reaction to the trauma of being discharged.

The Challenger Index of Job Search Statistics shows that the number of discharged managers who decide to start their own businesses has dropped slightly since the middle of the decade, going from about 11 percent in 1995 to about 7 percent in 1998. However, of those who did start their own businesses during that period, on average 80 percent were over the age of 40.

Outsourcing

As departments have disbanded, downsized, or combined, the trend toward contracting work out has grown appreciably. With smaller staffs, many corporations turn to entrepreneurs and consultants to provide specialized services.

Second Income from a Spouse

Launching a business meant considerable family sacrifice in the days when only the head of household worked. For years, in fact, entrepreneurship was often reserved for those who were single, because they did not have the constraints of married life and children restricting their expenditures or schedules.

Today, a working spouse's income provides an important financial cushion. The married person who can count on a second income to pay bills and meet living expenses is relieved of much of the financial insecurity that once stopped would-be entrepreneurs.

Computer Technology

The computer has dramatically expanded opportunities to operate a business successfully. It lets a sole proprietor or a small entrepreneurial team create and manage records that once required an army of file clerks. Through the Internet, it enables a tiny company to sell its products to the world. It can even be used to design and test products. The computer's versatility has enabled untold millions to launch businesses that could not have been conceived of even a decade ago.

Role Models and Support

Finally, entrepreneurship gets great press. The American tradition of the self-made man or woman fits beautifully with legends of businesses that start in a garage and end up earning billions in an initial public offering. Quieter examples also are influential. Almost everyone knows someone who has "gone out on his own." High-profile examples in the media and low-profile examples down the street add up to a wealth of role models and support for anyone contemplating an entrepreneurial venture.

What It Takes to Be an Entrepreneur

Entrepreneurship is not for everyone. Entrepreneurs exude a willingness to take risks and typically have high levels of energy and drive. They also tend to be creative thinkers who have proven leadership ability and a strong foundation of business expertise.

Whether you want to start a new venture, buy a small business or franchise, or begin consulting in your area of expertise, the following criteria are necessary for success.

Commitment

Starting a business takes a substantial commitment of time and personal effort. It is a time-and-a-half job, not a part-time job. Your business must come first. You will have less time for family and personal activities—and less money, too. Before you decide to go out on your own, make sure you are willing to make these sacrifices and stick with your business goal no matter what.

A Sound Financial Plan

Starting a business takes money, and income can be uncertain. Before you invest time and money in a venture that may not support you, take the time to draw up a financial plan. Use it to determine how much equity and working capital you will need, and to project income and expenses for several years. When you are on a payroll, stockholders and owners assume the financial risk. When you are in charge, your money is on the table. Protect your assets and income by doing your homework up front.

A Solid Track Record

A common mistake among would-be entrepreneurs is venturing into a new field in which they have no experience. Just as I counsel people not to change careers when they seek new employment, I counsel people who want to start businesses to stick with what they know. Trying something different—including the purchase of a franchise about which you know nothing—only increases your chances of failure, because you would be competing with others who have more experience.

There are exceptions. Some people have successfully adapted to a different field, but the percentage is small compared to those who could not adapt. Within the framework of your own knowledge and expertise, ask yourself, "Where is a need in the marketplace that I can serve?"

Sales Experience

As an entrepreneur, you should expect to spend 75 percent or more of your time on sales as the business is getting off the ground. *If you do not feel comfortable selling, your business is probably doomed before it even begins.* No business can succeed without sales. A strong sales commitment is necessary, especially in the first 12 to 24 months. This sales effort is not something you can delegate. You are the owner, the one with the vision and the stake in the business. If you leave selling to someone else, the vision will not be as compelling and your stake will be at risk. If you want to be a manager, get a job. If you are willing to sell, then and only then can you make your own business successful.

Stamina

Starting a new business takes stamina—the energy to withstand the physical rigors of starting up and operating a business. Because stamina is so important, entrepreneurship has long been considered a venture for the young. But more and more aging baby boomers are becoming entrepreneurs. In 1998, 84 percent of all those starting up their own businesses were over 40 compared with an average of 64 percent in 1991. As I mentioned at the outset of this book, today's experienced workers, particularly those over 50, are healthier and feel and look younger than their counterparts even 20 years ago. Still, you need to assess whether you are up to the challenge of long hours and long periods of uncertainty.

Not Everyone Is Right for Self-Employment

Owning a business is the dream of many, but at Challenger, Gray & Christmas, we sometimes talk clients out of that dream. For example, one dischargee had spent the majority of his business career as a midlevel manager with a large corporation. When that company was merged with another major firm, the combined entity required fewer people in his area so he was one of those discharged. When he arrived for outplacement counseling, he expressed a desire to start his own business rather than attempt to get back on another payroll. He felt that his extensive business background and MBA from a leading university would qualify him well for entrepreneurship.

This client wanted to start up a manufacturing supply business. However, it became apparent in conversations with him that he had no previous experience in that area and no idea of how much money it would take to start the business and keep it operating until it became profitable. Moreover, he had no previous sales experience, having been a manager in all of his previous positions.

Our counselor recommended that this client not pursue starting his own company. It is unfortunate to dash someone's hopes and aspirations, but he was simply not qualified for entrepreneurship.

Consulting: An Attractive Alternative

As outsourcing becomes a common means to reduce corporate overhead and operating expenses, demand for consultants and service industries is growing. A whole new breed of consultants is serving former industries and even former employers on a per-project basis. Companies welcome them because these consultants speak their language. They know their industry and require little or no training or orientation time.

There is a ready market for services, often from former employers, but only if you make an effort to sell them your skills. What sweet economic revenge: getting hired by an employer who let you go to do the same or similar job!

Some people use consulting as a means of getting back on the company payroll. Done well, it can showcase your talents and enable you to "shop" the company looking for permanent job opportunities. However, if you intend to pursue consulting as a career, you will need to use a contract from a former employer as a launching pad to more business with new clients. Too many consultants rely wholly on their former employer and find themselves without other clients or prospects when their contract is cancelled.

Although consulting offers a happy medium between launching a capital-intensive business and returning to corporate employment, it is still a business venture. You are no longer an employee. You are a business owner. You need to sell your services to new prospects, and you need to price your services to cover your bottom line and provide sufficient income for you and your family.

A New Trend: Retiree-Entrepreneurs

Thanks to buyouts and other early retirement policies, the first of 78 million baby boomers will begin to leave the workplace early in the next century. I believe that many will not be ready to spend their days playing golf or babysitting grandchildren. Confident in their business skills and abilities, a tidal wave of "seniorpreneurs" will break over the employment scene. Some of these seniorpreneurs will work for increased financial security. Others will go into business because they love their work and the recognition and satisfaction it brings.

The possibilities for retiree-entrepreneurships are virtually limitless. After spending decades on someone else's payroll, many retirees will realize they have accumulated the know-how to run an operation in a similar company. Others may expand a hobby into a money-making venture or join forces with family members to open a business.

These retiree-run enterpreneurships will be a boon to older job hunters. Entrepreneurial ventures need employees with extensive previous experience—individuals who need little or no training and can help the business turn a profit quickly. In addition, employers hire people they like and with whom they feel a common bond. Older business owners will hire an older workforce.

I forecast that "seniorpreneurships" with a majority of older employees will spring up around the country. These companies will be highly competitive due to their employees' years of experience and valuable business contacts. Their workforce also will be more stable, because older employees are far less likely to move from job to job.

Businesses run by retirees will spin age discrimination in a new direction. It may result in employees in their twenties, thirties, or even forties charging unfairness and denial of career opportunities because they believe they are perceived as too young and inexperienced to do the job. Ideally, retiree-entrepreneurship will not drive a wedge between the generations but will become fertile ground for mentoring and skill development. Businesses owned and operated by a majority of older people will have a responsibility for guiding the career paths of younger employees.

Retiree-entrepreneurs have much to offer the workplace and their impact will increasingly be felt in the coming years.

The Rewards of Entrepreneuring

Those with the vision and the know-how to create a business earn two incomes: the paycheck they deposit, and the psychic income they enjoy. As an entrepreneur, you are in effect the captain of your own ship, making your own decisions, not having to clear anything with anyone other than your customers. You can put your own ideas into effect and do things the way you think they should be done. When you succeed, you can enjoy freedom, independence, and the personal satisfaction of knowing that you are the one who made it happen.

However, many more people consider entrepreneurship than actually embrace it. Among Challenger, Gray & Christmas clients, the great majority opt for returning to a payroll in the end. Both decisions are valid. My advice is to pursue the avenue that fits you best. You need to make an honest and comprehensive assessment of your potential and not mislead yourself into making an inappropriate choice.

Is Entrepreneurship for You?

To successfully launch a new business venture, you need to be able to answer "yes" to each of the following questions:

- Do you have a second income you can count on?

- Can you put your business before everything else, including family?

- Do you have (or can you raise) sufficient start-up money and working capital?

- Are you experienced in this area?

- Do you have the stamina to work long hours and endure long periods of uncertainty?

- Are you comfortable selling?

About the Author

JAMES E. CHALLENGER is president of Challenger, Gray & Christmas, Inc., an international outplacement consulting firm. He is considered the nation's foremost authority on finding new employment and has frequently been quoted in the nation's media. He graduated from Harvard University with an A.B. degree and obtained his J.D. degree from Northwestern University Law School. He has served as president and/or senior partner of Challenger, Gray & Christmas, Inc. and its predecessor partnership since its inception. The company maintains more than 30 regional offices in the United States, Canada, and internationally.